Past Due

How To Make Money Investing in Non
Performing Real Estate Mortgage Notes

Matthew Hell

Making Money Investing in Non Performing Real Estate Mortgage Notes

Matthew Hell

Copyright 2016

First Edition

www.MatthewHell.com/BookBonus

2016

DEDICATION

I dedicate this book to my real estate mentors for their time to help me achieve success in this business. Along with my mentors, I would like to extend an appreciation to my parents, Sheree and Doug Hell, for their loving support while I learned from each trial and error. These trial and errors taught me everything I know and have the pleasure to teach.

I would like to thank my students for allowing me to guide you with valuable insight and give you the steps to change your life not only financially but emotionally and too. Lastly, I would like to extend gratitude towards: Robert Kiyosaki, Ron Legrand, Eddie Speed, Robyn Thompson, Gordon Moss, Dave Vanhorn, Bob Paulous and Dave Ramsey and countless other individuals for sharing your insights with me.

CONTENTS

ACKNOWLEDGEMENTS

I want to start by thanking all of my previous mentors and friends: my parents Doug and Sheree Hell, brother Mitchell Hell, Zoey Dexter, and Laura DeLestry. These individuals ignited a spark to motivate and support me throughout my career. I cannot explain how blessed I feel for the lessons, talks, and time they have spent to allow me to build my business. They will always be my mastermind and support team.

I would like to extend an acknowledgement of thankfulness to my first inspiration to break free of the rat race and look towards real estate investing: **Robert Kiyosaki.** Kiyosaki's book *Rich Dad, Poor Dad* allowed me to see diagrams and information that breaks down steps so that anyone can have financial independence. His book is a must read to everyone interested in learning the basics of financial literacy. I am honored to be mentored by him.

Next, I would like to thank **Ron Legrand**. According to the Minnesota Real Estate Investor's Association, Legrand is "the legendary coach in real estate all across America and Canada," (2010) because he has taught thousands of individuals how to become financially free investing in real estate. One of the reasons I respect Legrand is due to his honesty with mistakes. He always lets his mentees know about mistakes he has made so they do not duplicate them in their professional world. Legrand has a mentality to *tell it like it is* which supercharged all my facets in real estate investing.

For example when we talk with motivated sellers, we get right to the point and lead them in the direction that would help their situation best. Legrand is an excellent resource which I, as well as multiple others, look up to.

Another person I would like to personally acknowledge is **Eddie Speed**. He has helped me not only as a mentor but also with negotiating skills to buy multiple non performing and performing notes. Speed developed Note School several years ago and his lessons have enhanced my learning by giving numerous techniques to finding notes and working out positive solutions with homeowners across the country. Another valuable resources has been his book Streetwise Seller Financing. This book is the only book you will need to put together deals when creating seller financed notes. Speed is an essential resource for every new note investor.

Robyn Thompson, what a lady she is, still the best dressed in all of her classes. Robyn has inspired my brother and I to dive into some rehab projects when we first started and your guidance on the scope of work and working with "Mature Grown-Up Adults" make our projects a huge success. It pays to learn from the *Queen of Rehab* because she have done it all, and we love what she has to offer and instilled in my brother and me. We avidly use all the direct mail pieces, especially the *yellow letter*; these direct mail pieces provide the very best rate of return of any direct marketing piece. Blessings go out to Robyn and your horse farm in FL.

Gordon Moss, and his brother, John, remind me of my brother and I, just a bit senior. Gordon has taught me how incredibly easy and passive this business really is. I was nervous at first for dealing in this niche especially with bankruptcy and foreclosure, but his teachings smoothed those opportunities out. He has inspired me not to deal with tenants and toilets anymore. It's really a pain when you're on vacation in Mexico and someone from one of your rentals says, yah, I think we broke the toilet, can you come over? We don't have to do that anymore, just dealing with legit people and helping them pay off their liens.

Dave VanHorn and Bob Paulous, The whole gang at Partners for Payment Relief rock! I appreciate the way Dave started with credit cards to start his career in real estate. Bob has the most amazing posture when talking with homeowners, and my brother and I aspire to be just like that, we are getting very close by the way. Partners for Payment Relief is where we received our training for Performing and Nonperforming Notes and we are so glad we did. The hedge fund is amazing and love receiving collateral files in the mail. They are so nicely organized and I'm like a kid on Christmas day when receiving them.

Dave Ramsey, *Financial Peace University* is one of the most valuable courses everyone should go through. I love listening to the radio show each morning and continually learning from Ramsey Studios wealth of knowledge. I discovered the radio show and teachings through a trusted friend and mentor *Josh Dexter*, and never regretted it. Dave's books are truthful and the right way to build wealth and sustain it for future generations. My Brother and I teach *Financial Peace University* courses to our local churches and spread your tips and techniques in blasting debt out of their lives. I gave myself a "plasticectamy" years ago, and would never go back!

A special thanks to my brother, **Mitchell Hell** who has tirelessly worked with me through our entire journey in real estate investing. I like to refer to him as the tech guy, creating all the website stuff that I don't understand to say the least. He has created our systems and all the background operations. Thanks for making mistakes with me and being by my side. Cheers to the future we created and to the endless opportunities and fun we have ahead of us. It was so worth all the trials, tribulations and failures we've crushed and overcame. I'm excited to start a family and do things with them that we were never able to. **Let's go travel the world, we've earned it!**

INTRODUCTION

A Crash Course in Sharing my Story
It is so Cold, am I Still Alive?

I was traveling down Highway 94 from Eau Claire, Wisconsin to Minneapolis, Minnesota on the morning of February 11, 2013. As I drove I wondered what caused the stars to twinkle the way they do even in the cold and if they are outside all day where can I not see them in daylight? While everything on Earth hunkers down in negative degree weather they somehow find the strength to dance in front of you. Focus, I thought, watch the road, it is negative twenty-two degrees out and anything can happen.

I continued driving along at a steady speed and all of a sudden two bright lights of an eighteen wheel semi truck came behind me and rammed me while I was going 65 miles per hour. My car started to slide, I could not see. Each star sketched in my head brought forth a memory from my life. While I watched my life flash before my eyes I could hear the tires scraping the rumble strips in the road as I bounced from the right to left lane. I was face to face going straight into an icy ditch when a guardian angel stopped my car and pulled me over to the right side of the highway. It must have been a dream.

I widened my eyes to blinding lights. *Stars? Heaven?* Looking down, I saw the semi with only a few dents. Yet my Toyota Prius had glass shattered throughout it, everywhere. The door was smashed in and the windows were busted into hundreds of pieces.

I could feel the temperature inside the car degreasing. My head hurt from impact and my neck was too stiff to move it. A wet substance fell from my chin to my lap, it was red. I survived the crash but knew I would not survive the cold without help. I started to pray.

A few minutes later flashing lights appeared off in the distance, I had a glimmer of hope. Four emergency technicians ran out to see what had happened. Within minutes I was in a neck brace and carefully placed on a moveable cot and wheeled into the back of the rig.

Promptly, we arrived at the emergency room where I was taken care of. After all the tests were finished the doctors told me I was lucky to be walking away with only a neck brace. What they did not understand is that I was not leaving with only support for neck but a new outlook on life.

I realized all those stars I looked so carefully before are always there but unless you look for them you will not find them. The crazy thing about life is its constantly in motion. At some point it becomes your job to take charge of your life. You are responsible to do, see, and be anything or anyone you dream of. If I was too pass away when I did I would die without satisfaction.

So many individuals are stuck in a job that limits theirself to a small portion of what they really want to do. I cannot say for you, but when I pass away I want people to know that I mattered and made a difference on other's lives around me. You are not guaranteed tomorrow and do not know what the future holds. When you reflect back at your life do you want to think of all the events you missed out of because of work? According to the Washington Post "87% of individuals do not enjoy going to their profession." Are you one of them?

I am presenting you this information to expose you to a new idea of creating passive. Passive income is money coming in each month without you having to work strenuous hours to receive it. This income allows you to enjoy whatever is most important in your life without the stress of showing up for work. If this interests you, please keep reading to find out how to create multiple, reliable, income streams that will eventually allow you to separate from your J.O.B. (Just Over Broke) if you would like and life the life you deserve.

CHAPTER ONE

WHAT IS YOUR "WHY?"

"It's time to start living the life you've imagined."

-Henry James

To begin, I would like to thank you for purchasing my book and want to congratulate yourself on taking the next step to improve your future and financial independance. Before we can begin, you need to know that being successful at real estate starts between your two ears. That's right, it is your mindset. Once you can think in terms of abundance and see opportunity than you are read to grasp it.

I have been a part of multiple different corporations working but never found any of them fulfilling. Although I really enjoyed working I did not feel that my job offered a deeper meaning. I, like many other entrepreneurs, understood that having a traditional J.O.B. (just over broke) would not cut it. As Robert Kiyosaki would say, most individuals are in a *Rat Race.*

A typical rat race consists of getting up early, eating a quick breakfast, commuting to a job so that someone or something else profits, come home exhausted, spend a short time with family, and then go to bed to begin this process the next four days straight.

I want you to have something to look forward to. Some people do not mind working such a fast paced job everyday for several years, but many have trouble doing this. They need opportunities, and I will help you reach them.

This journey was not get rich quick either as it took nearly four and a half years to get where we are as of this writing. I remember countless times where we struggled to get it right. We pulled numerous all nighters brainstorming and figuring out ways to pull this this real estate endeavor off. It took many years to establish a credible name in the industry the trust of my numerous clients. Now that I have it, it was all worth the hardships, trials and errors.

My journey was difficult and took a long time. I can remember countless times my brother, Mitchell, and I struggled to get things right. We pulled numerous all nighters brainstorming new ways to pull our real estate endeavor off. It took multiple years to establish a credible name in the industry and to receive the trust of numerous clients. Now that Mitchell and I have it, it was worth the hardship, trials and errors.

Discovering your why...

About five years ago from the date of this writing, as you had just read, I had fell victim to a terrible accident. I had decided that family and helping others in hard situations were the most important things to me and that I wanted to learn

6

how to create an income, an income that provides money monthly and could be reliable without having to physically work a job.

I will be asking you a series of questions below. When first starting in this industry, my mentor asked me similar questions and really wanted me to determine my "Why."

Your "why" is the entire reason you are doing what you are doing. Your why could be you want to quit your job to enjoy more time with your friends and family. Another could be is that you love to help people solve problems and you would gladly accept some extra money on the side.

The value of having a strong why is that when things get tough, and they will, you will get through it because you have a bigger purpose in your life. You have a "why" to achieve, whatever that may be. Things will happen, you will get kicked down, and then again, but you need to get back up and start back on your journey. Your why will keep you motivated. So let's get started on these questions.

I want you to answer a few questions alone. The purpose of you figuring out these questions without distractions is to unlock your subconscious mind where many of your thoughts form and can be rooted and expanded on. Please write down your answers on the lines below.

Question 1.

Do you feel the lack of money or abundant in money? Why do you feel this way?

When answering this question, think about all the reasons why you feel the way you do. The easiest way to do this is to listen and watch your thoughts when you start to think about money. What is your mind telling you? How do you feel when thinking about money?

_____

_____

_____

_____

_____

_____

_____

_____

_____

Question 2.

Do you think you deserve money, lots of it, enough to change your life and others?

_____

_____

_____

_____

_____

_____

_____

_____

_____

_____

Question 3.

How would having an abundance of money and time affect you and people you love?

Think to yourself what it would be like if I gave you the exact amount of money you wanted. How would it feel? What would you do? How would your life change?

_____

_____

_____

_____

_____

_____

_____

_____

_____

_____

Question 4.

How would you spend this money that is coming to you? Examples, Travel, spend time with family, build an orphanage in Africa, go on missions trips? You need to know what you want, only then will you receive the money in the right proportions to do what you want.

_____

_____

_____

_____

_____

_____

_____

_____

_____

_____

Will you commit to reading the rest of this book and learning how to create financial freedom as my brother, Mitchell, and I did?

(Write Yes if **BIG BOLD LETTERS Right HERE**→)

You see, by answering these questions, you are digging deep down into the part of your mind where all your intimate details rest. Everything you have ever learned or experienced, either positive or negative, is all stored there. This is referred to your subconscious mind. This is where you will need to look deeply into because it is where all your beliefs and predispositions come from. We need to correct this and rewrite what you negative beliefs you may have about money.

When my Mitch, my brother, and I started in real estate long ago, we were in a poor and lack mentality, it was as if we never had enough money. Usually, we made the money in our deals, but then it was gone. We wondered why we didn't have any at the end of the year.

It was because we spent it on the little stuff, worthless stuff that would never increase in value. It wasn't until we were mentored by wealthy people that we understood to only buy things that increased in value.

I remember when I received a huge check from a deal in Minneapolis, and I leased my first new car. I thought it was a good idea at the time. Driving a new flashy car wasn't so bad until I learned I was actually renting the car, had a certain amount of miles I could use, and the down payment I put on it, I'd never get back. And to top things off, I had to return the car in two years. This was a wakeup call. Lesson learned; buy your cars in cash, only what you can afford. I can tell you that most millionaires drive two year old used cars and only until you have a net worth of one million dollars should you purchase a new car.

Learning how the wealthy think, and act towards money is one of the most valuable things we have ever learned in this endeavor. In order to build and sustain wealth for your future generations you must learn to master money, make every dollar work for you.

Think of money like employees, no one likes when employees stand around and do nothing. Make them work for you; place them in investments that will make you money. Do you like working for your money, or do you want your money to work for you? Millionaires like money working for them. You have to make that choice.

What's Your Why

You must have a "Why" if you want to make a huge change in your life. Ask yourself why are you reading this book about how to create financial freedom. Why do you want to make a change? You must figure you the why because that reason will carry you through the tough times any business will bring your way.

My "Why" is my family, and home. I want to create an amazing life for them. I want to give them all the opportunities and possibilities to fully enjoy life. I want to have the time to spend with my kids, watch them grow up and create the best memories. I want to have the most incredible relationship with my future wife, create a fulfilling, romantic, and intimate bond and share our life together.

Owning my own home has always been one of my biggest goals, the amazing part is this business is going to allow me to do that. I've always wanted a home with a nice yard for my family to enjoy. It's nice to know that helping homeowners stay in their homes will let me enjoy my dream home. This is what keeps me motivated day in and day out. It is all for my family.

Let's make this first chapter hit home. You need to want to make a change in your life and set a deliberate desire to make this valuable information supplied here to you to work. I don't want you to read any further if you are not serious about changing your life.

If you are serious, let's take a journey step by step to create financial abundance with this training and I am so very excited for you to finish this book and help so many people out while helping yourself. I will love to hear your success stories and how your life has changed while implementing this information that has been provided to you. You will be able to share your experiences at MatthewHell.com/successstories.

For an incredible read after this book, Check out my brother's book: *Choice of Freedom: The 11 Principles To Break Free From Your J.O.B, Design Your Own Lifestyle and Enjoy a Life of Freedom and Abundance* on Amazon

by Mitchell Hell

CHAPTER TWO

CREATING FINANCIAL FREEDOM FROM REAL ESTATE NOTES

"Success is the sum of small efforts, repeated day in and day out"

-Robert Collier

You may be wondering what a note or lien is. Basically, a note / lien is a *promise to pay.* We have all worked with notes for most of our lives. Take out a dollar bill from your wallet right now and look at the top where it says "Federal Reserve Note." That means that we exchange currency (fiat money) and it is backed by the full faith and credit of the United States Treasury.

Another example are checks. Checks are also a form of a note. Whenever you write or receive a check from a business or person, that specific entity is writing an I.O.U. (I owe you money) to you, backed by their currency in their bank account.

So, now that you are more familiar to what a note is let's dive deeper into what real estate notes are. Real Estate notes are an I.O.U. from a buyer to the lender. The buyer borrows money from the lender for a real estate property. In order to complete this transaction, a note and mortgage is created.

The note is the I.O.U. on the money borrowed, while the mortgage is the collateral on the loan which would be the property itself.

If ever the buyer were to default or get behind on payments to the lender, the lender could use the house as collateral, also known as the mortgage, to recoup some of the lost funds involved in the transaction. For example, Mark, a middle aged man, loses his job and can't pay anymore on this loan. Mark agreed to pay the bank at the time the note was issued and the bank will hold his home as collateral if Mark stops paying. Eventually, the bank will foreclose on the home and re sell it to recoup their funds originally owed from Mark.

Notes can be Non Performing (NPF) or Performing Notes (PN). A **non performing note** is when the borrower stops paying on the note and a performing note is when the lender is receiving payments. I will also be calling these **liens**, one of the following, non performing second position liens, non performing junior liens, or non performing seconds, or notes. They are all the same, often times said differently depending on the person talking about them. Don't worry if these terms confuse you right now, I will explain them in the coming chapters.

When you think of buying a home, you will most likely need to take out a loan from the bank right? This loan will usually include closing costs and other miscellaneous fees included in it. We will call this the senior lien because it's the biggest lien on the home and it's the first loan taken out on the home.

In some cases, the homeowner may not have enough money to cover the down payment; most banks want at least 20% down to qualify for a home loan. The homeowner now needs to take out some more money from another bank to cover the rest of the down payment for the bank. This loan is called the junior lien or second position lien. It is smaller than the senior loan.

So how does a note go *non performing*? Let's say Bill, a regular and hardworking guy, purchases a home, but he doesn't have enough of a down payment to pay the full amount the primary bank needs for their requirements. Bill will need to go to another bank and request a small loan and add that to the remaining down payment for this home. He gets qualified for the home, and all is well.

Five years later, Bill gets sick, and his wife is a stay at home mother. John decides to stop paying on the smaller loan he needed for his initial down payment, but he keeps paying his senior mortgage on the property. In Bill's mind, he thought he needed to pay other expenses for some reason. In essence, Bill stopped paying the junior lien and the note is no longer performing because he can't afford to pay it.

There's another case where this may happen too. For example, Betsy has only one loan on her home, but she wants to do some remodeling. So, Betsy heads to her local bank and takes out a HELOC (Home Equity Line of Credit) for the remodel of her kitchen. The next winter, Betsy betsy contracts an infection from visiting the Amazon on missions trip. Because of the extent of her infection, she needs to be laid of work for two months without income.

Unfortunately, Betsy can't pay on her second mortgage and goes into default on the junior lien.

Why Junior Liens?

Why would you be interested in investing in non performing junior liens? When I say non performing, I am referring to a lien that is not being paid. The example I shared above features a hard situation that hits a home owner, in this scenario they may not be able to pay both liens. So they may stop paying one which is usually the second or junior lien.

Although homeowners stop paying the junior lien, there is an opportunity to make a lot of money from helping homeowners repay their debts. It feels incredibly satisfying to make lots of money and help someone stay in their home; likewise, being the person to help others who have nowhere to turn trust you to make a positive change in their life.

We continue to have positive relationships with numerous past homeowners whose homes we have owned notes for. Each client is appreciative when they know that on the other end of the phone, they have someone to speak with who will try their best to understand them and their unique situation. I believe there is no better business than this one where you can make such a substantial impact on someone's life.

Although there is a degree of risk, these junior liens are a superb way for a beginner investor to get their feet wet when entering the real estate investing arena. These liens are non performing, which means if the buyer has defaulted on paying; the lien can be bought for less than half the cost.

In summary this means, you can purchase these liens for half or less of their full face value because they are delinquent. I have built up strong relationships with a few private hedge funds around the country and can purchase them at nearly 20% of their face value, the price the note was originally written for. This is due to hedge funds being a collective group of investors who buy assets from a bank for a cheap rate and resell these assets for a markup.

For example, if the note has a face value of $100,000, I could buy the note for $20,000. That would mean I would receive $80,000 worth of equity at the time of purchase.

A hedge fund is a collective group of large investors who have a lot of cash to invest in numerous assets. The hedge fund we purchase our notes from is called *Partners for Payments Relief* in Pennsylvania. I will mention them again later in this book, but for now let's focus on how hedge funds work.

Remember when we had the huge fiasco sub prime mortgage crisis in 2007 -2009? Banks were lending to anyone who had some credit, and as they say "whomever could fog a mirror." This expression essentially says that people who definitely could not afford a mortgage payment easily received the signed paperwork for their dream homes. Eventually, the bills caught up to them and they could not pay anymore, the bank took back their property and the homeowner went into foreclosure.

Banks are not in the business of taking properties back. Banks are in the business of lending. The interest people pay on bank loans is the real money maker along with products and services provided by the banks. When a bank acquires a property back, they need to pay all the costs of owning the estate. This can be a fairly large number depending on the size and location of the property.

When a bank takes back several properties, it does not look well on their books, from a company or government regulatory standpoint. Banks would rather sell these assets at a loss than to keep them on their books and remain making payments towards these reality. Banks will sell these homes for pennies on the dollar to rejuvenate money fast.

Giant hedge funds are perfect buyers for these assets; they will literally approach banks and ask to see their portfolio of non- performing assets. Hedge funds will pay cash for these sums of assets and then will resell them to people like you and I for a small spread. This is how they make their money and how we can gain access to these gems.

The best way to find quality hedge funds, and I will list the ones I currently use, is to build quality relationships with people who are actually in real estate business every day. They have "boots on the ground" and "work in the trenches."

Let me give you a $15,000.00 tip. Never buy notes from eBay or "joker brokers." I did this in the past and had a mountain of issues that added up to the nearly 15k in un-needed expenses.

I actively purchase notes from Partners for Payment Relief. http://pprnoteco.com

Realized Profit Margins

Let's get into the fun stuff and learn how much you can make with some real life examples.

Each month, I look at a "pool" of notes that a hedge fund is selling. The pool is a collection of delinquent notes that hedge funds sell. Hedge funds will periodically send out an excel spreadsheet called a "tape." You can pick and choose from this tape which loans catch your eye. For example if one catches our eye and it only costs $12,400.00 to purchase we will do our due diligence or research on the loan, in which we will discuss how to do in the next few chapters, before we make a buying decision.

In this example the note costs $12,400.00 and we will assume it has a 9.8% interest rate attached to it. The interest rate tells is how much interest in written into the loan.

Let's also assume the homeowner got sick four years ago and had not been paying for four years.

The face value of the loan is $49,000.00 in which the tape would state and payments are 397.10. Face value means what the loan was written out for or the total amount the borrower owes you.

Face Value:	**$49,000.00**
Payment (PMT) :	**$397.10**
Interest Rate:	**9.8 %**
Note Costs:	**$12,400.00**
Unpaid Principal Balance	**(UPB)$ 48,624.12**

In this example, I am paying around 30 cents on the dollar for this note. In ideal circumstances, I will work out with the buyer to pay me the arrears (back payments). Back payments are the payments the homeowner has been delayed on. They are the payments they still owe. I will then discuss what they can afford to pay me each month, ideally $397.00 or whatever the borrower can afford.

Let's break this down more, you paid around twelve thousand dollars for this loan, they still owe you around 36,224.00. That's the difference from the unpaid principal balance and the amount you paid for the note. You ask the borrower what they can afford each month, they say they can pay you $350.00 and can pay you $10,000.00 towards the principal balance this month. In other words, they will pay you around eighty percent what you paid for their loan and you will receive $350.00 per month until paid.

Any moneys collected after the amount you paid for the loan will be pure profit on this asset. Because you own the loan, asking the borrower how much they can afford will benefit both you and them. You can negotiate the price as long as it works for both parties. If the borrower is having difficulty with the payment, I usually make the payment at least twenty five percent of their take home income. That way they will remain paying you because they have an extra cushion for their other expenses. Some of our friends didn't budge on the payment for the borrower and had a terrible time collecting payments simply because the borrower could not afford to pay them.

As long as you work the with homeowner and adjust to their needs with payments and the larger amounts they owe you, there is a high chance you will make out well in these deals.

Can you see the financial potential in these notes and how much leverage they can give you? Are you starting to see how these can change your life and outlook on it. I saw this right away and jumped on the opportunity to buy these the very next day.

You may be telling yourself right now, Matthew, I don't have that much money to spend on notes! I will say that when we first started, we only had $2000.00 to spend on a note. My brother and I split the cost and pulled from our savings account. The loan was really beat up, but we were able to workout a solution with the homeowner and put that money towards more notes. We made nearly a $7000.00 profit after all expenses!

The next step is to put away money each month to purchase your note. I would strongly recommend you have at least $10,000.00 liquid funds to spend on notes getting started. This way, you can purchase a quality note for around five thousand dollars, and have an allotted amount to work with if you have to foreclose or service the loan in a particular way. I'm not saying you will spend the full ten thousand dollars but it's best to have it liquid, or ready to access, if you ever did need to use it.

Be one of the top two percent of successful people and keep reading to see why I'm crazy about these notes and you will be too!

CHAPTER THREE

WHY I AM CRAZY ABOUT NON PERFORMING JUNIOR LIENS

"If you are not willing to risk the usual, you will have to settle for the ordinary."

–Jim Rohn

I f you are like me, constantly busy, then you understand it is ideal not have to put a lot of work into something and still receive fantastic results in return.

If worked correctly, this lucrative business will provide you will with a form passive income and spurts of large revenue from collecting the arrears (again the back payments). In some cases, you may need to exercise your legal right to foreclose on the residence and obtain a physical property. We will discuss these legal actions in much more detail in the foreclosure chapter.

I want to share with you why I like these junior liens. First, I can buy these loans in the comfort of my own home. You see, each month I receive a tape (spreadsheet) of loans to choose from my hedge funds. I pick which individual loans or pools I like and do some simple systematized research, in which we will discuss in Chapter five. Submit an offer, buy, and receive the collateral file in the mail the next day.

When I mention "collateral file" this means you will receive the original paperwork such as the mortgage or deed of trust, note, and any other pertinent information regarding the specific property. You will need to sign a confidentiality agreement with the hedge fund because you will be working with people's social security numbers and they only want to work with trustworthy investors. All you have to do is register to become a new note buyer, fill in some personal information, and wait for a response from the company that sells the notes.

The freedom of buying these liens from anywhere gives you the opportunity for complete freedom of where you want to live. That is what drew me to this investment vehicle. You can literally live anywhere in the world and still have the ability to work with the homeowner. One of the big misconceptions with working with these liens is that you have to buy them where you live. First, the chances of you obtaining notes where you live are small. Second, you own the loan, not the property, or at least not just yet.

Cash Flow

When you work with a homeowner, you need to work out a solution so they can pay you a manageable amount every month. This in return creates a cash flow or a stream of income for yourself. When you want to make note investing your full time income, you will need multiple streams of income to replace your current career income. When you develop a substantial portfolio of notes, you can make the final decision to fire your boss.

Lets say you make an average annual salary of $30,000/YR. And, you want to replace your income within five years with note investing. Knowing the average lien will pay about $200.00-$450.00 per month, how many liens do you need performing to replace your income?

Your Current Yearly salary $30,000.00

Your Current Monthly Salary $2,500.00

How many performing notes will you need to replace your monthly salary?

$2500.00 / ($450.00 High Note Payment)   = 6 Notes (rounded up)

You only need 6 performing notes paying you an average of $450.00 per month to replace your current monthly income

Can you start to see how these numbers can add up? It is exciting to know that breaking it down, creates a much easier and doable plan.

No Tenants and Toilets

When you own notes on homes, you are dealing with homeowners, not tenants. The homeowner is responsible for all maintenance and repairs on their home. They are on the deed to the property making them liable for utilities. Owning the note, you just own the "I owe you" on the property, in which they legally have to pay you, and in some cases you will have the right to foreclose on the property for nonpayment.

The nice part about knowing you are not responsible for the utilities is that, you do not have to worry about tenant complaints, snow removal, roof repair, clogged toilets, etc. One of the biggest reasons I got out of rentals was I was tired of getting calls on holidays saying, " Hi, we accidently flushed the toothpaste tube down the toilet and it won't flush anymore, and by the way, there is a border line backing up to on the floor." Who in their right mind wants to get calls like this, especially when you are with your family or spouse? Owning the loan, you will not have to deal with this.

My brother and I dabbled in the rental industry in a small college house with a few partners and experienced what it means to be landlords. We rented to primarily the student population and had some eye opening experiences.

There was one time we witnessed one of our tenants having a party at our rental that we owned. We even saw one punk in back of the home spraying paint onto the white siding. That sure ended fast, we know we did not want to deal directly with the home, and quickly shifted our strategy to owning the loan on the homes.

Creating Time Freedom

Let me ask you some serious questions. Are you chained to your job? Do you want to go to work tomorrow? Do you even like your job?

I was asked these very questions when first starting in non performing junior liens. They really struck a chord in me and answered "no" to two of the three of the questions.

Could you leave your current position if a family member needed you right now in the hospital? The majority of people could not leave, or they would be reprimanded for leaving. Did you know as of the time of this writing, living in America the richest country in the world, 76% of Americans are living paycheck to paycheck?

Some people may have to take a vacation day just to see their loved one. Do you really want someone else to determine if you can see a family member in need? Think about that for a few minutes. Do you want to be in control of your financial life or have someone else control it? Make your decision now.

I knew when I was laid up in the hospital for the time I was in my accident, I had in the back of my mind all the menusha I had at work to do, schedules, payroll, etc. You should not need to think about these things when your life is on the line. The majority of the working class would think almost the same way.

You see, we all long for more time. It is the one thing that can not be replaced and when you really look back, spending time at your job and all the stress that comes with that **WILL NOT** matter. It will not be about your status or what material objects you have. Spending time with whom or what matters most to you will be first on your mind.

I made my decision, that my family is the most important aspect in my life. Family always comes first no matter what, no excuses. I always want to be there for my children and wife. This business has allowed me to always make time for what's most important.

For this next part, I will need you to put on your imagination hat. REALLY, go to a quiet place and think about this. Imagine right now as it is already happening that you can spend every holiday with your friends and family. You can spend the evening or mornings with your kids or pets, playing with them, spending quality time with them without stress from your job. You and your spouse can travel and go on vacation together, rekindling the relationship. This can be a reality for you!

Here are some questions I want you to answer by writing them out. Writing out your answers will make your intent clearer and feel as if it is so possible to attain. These questions are being presented to you as if you already are successful. Write your answers as if you are already doing this business. Be truthful to yourself.

Question 1.

I have an abundance of time and I like to spend it with... doing what?

_____

_____

_____

_____

_____

_____

_____

_____

_____

_____

Question 2.

What does it feel like to have this time freedom; I want you to write out your emotions?

_____

_____

_____

_____

_____

_____

_____

_____

_____

Question 3.

How does your outlook on life change knowing that you can do what you want, when you want?

_____

_____

_____

_____

_____

_____

_____

_____

_____

I hope you feel better after writing your answers down in this book. Keep in mind that your answers may change overtime due to different desires coming up in your life. You can always change them. I want you to feel inspired while imagining how life will be when you are successful. This is a learn by doing business, you will continue to gain experience the more borrowers you help. So take it easy on yourself when you first begin.

I want you to know that up to this point, you have been in control of your financial circumstances. You have the decision to take action to make money or not to. You have been in control the whole time.

You need to train your mind to start thinking in abundance and make your financial decisions from this mindset. Life is meant to be abundant; you need to choose to think this way though.

Lastly...Legal and Lawsuit Protection

Consult legal professional advice before pursuing, but I want to share what we have experienced.

When is the last time you heard of someone slipping on ice at a property and suing the bank for not shoveling or salting their walk ways? Almost never right? Being the "bank" and owning the note, you basically sidestep these situations.

Let me share a tip with you. We learned to place every note we bought into a separate entity, due to legal reasons. This tip has saved us in court battles many times. You have to think asset protection in this business. When you begin to make a lot of money, the more targets go on your back for legal lawsuits.

You can usually find where and how you can form your entity on your state's website.

For example we use the WI state website and form LLC's through: http://www.wdfi.org/apps/corpformation/directions.aspx?type=12

There are other ways to protect yourself legally, it's best to consult a real estate attorney to find out what type of protection works best for your strategy.

CHAPTER FOUR

HOW THESE NOTES WORK

*"Start where you are. Use what you have.
Do what you can."*

-Kevin Kline

It is time to talk about how and why these notes work. When speaking on stage at our live note mentoring events, understanding how these notes work can be one of the most challenging concepts for our attendees. They ask how one can make money from these investments and why would someone want to work with me. We are going to dive deep into how we operate and have been so successful at working our creative solutions with borrowers and making an absolute killing at it.

We will start with how we are different from banks and how the borrower notices. Have you ever taken out a loan at the bank? How did they treat you? Did they treat you like a number or a valued member benefiting their business?

Most banks will treat you in a non-personalized way as if you are just a number. There is not much personal contact, and if you were to default, there would definitely be nasty legal letters sent your way.

We treat our borrowers very differently and actually develop quality relationships with them. Ultimately, we want them to pay us a payment that they can afford along with all the arrears (back payments) they are obligated to pay on their loan.

You see, we will talk with the buyer, based on their situation, and discuss options on how they can pay off their loans. We will work with them; even modify their loan, so they can get back on track with their obligation. Our borrowers love us for this.

As the owner of the note, you have the ability to modify the loan in a way that suits you and the borrower. That is one of the best things about being the owner of the lien. You have the ability to solve the borrower's problem. Most of the time, the buyer does not pay because they do not know the loan can be modified. We have had countless cases where we discuss with the borrower what they can pay. We can even change the interest rate.

The way you separate yourself in this industry is to be different than anyone else. You need to be able to listen to the borrower. Hear their situation and be able to solve their problem. Trust me, when they know you are actually trying to help them, they will be so much more willing to work with you. This has been our experience with nearly every note.

Realize there will be some people who would rather have you out of their lives than to actually deal with their situation. You will have to send these people a demand letter (foreclosure letter) to let them know we are serious about legally pursuing your interest. Most times, after receiving the demand letter, the homeowners will work with you.

We once experienced a case where we were working with a person in Texas and he did not want to pay the high interest rate on the junior lien. We negotiated and asked him if he could raise his payment, we would lower the interest rate from 6.5% to 4.5%. In the big picture, we are creating more cash flow each month and the borrower is paying less on the interest rate on the loan. As you can see, you have numerous options to work out solutions with the borrowers.

Buyer Emotional Equity

Buyer emotional Equity is a term we frequently use in our practice and live events. When a buyer purchases a house, they may purchase it for an investment; however,in most cases they will purchase the home to start a family and or settle down.

The homeowners may have kids and gain roots in the community that they reside in and soon the house will become a home and memories are created. The borrower's family may find a church and schools to attend. The homeowners start to have a vested emotional tie to the property. How many of you have been in this situation?

Emotional equity is a key factor we look for when investing in notes. It usually means that the borrowers have a strong emotional tie to the property and the area and hope to continue staying there.

When purchasing notes, I look for if the senior lien is current and how much equity is their between the fair market value and the senior lien amount. In most cases, if the senior lien is current, meaning the borrower is still current on making payments to the larger loan, this kind of loan may be easier to work out a solution.

Fair market value of the home means how much the market would pay for the property in their area that it is located.

When the senior lien is current, the buyer shows that they want to stay in the property. When they want to stay at their home, you have a much better chance of contacting them and working out a solution. These notes may be a bit higher priced, but your return could be five times what you paid for the note. We have had several success stories from working a case where the senior lien is current.

Stay tuned to find out how to find these notes in the next chapter!

CHAPTER FIVE

FINDING, ANALYZING AND BUYING THE NOTES

Before you begin buying notes, you must know where to find them and what to look for. While you can purchase non performing notes from multiple sources, I am only going to give you the sources I buy mine from because I have built quality relationships over a number of years with specific people, institutions and hedge funds.

The Note Cycle

We are going to dive into the deep details how these notes are created. The note cycle flows as follows:

1. A lien is created
2. Next, the borrower stops paying, lien no longer performing
3. The lien is sold off
4. The lien is available for purchase (to large investors or hedge funds)
5. After that, the hedge fund sells lien to individual investor
6. Then, you and I buy these notes
7. Lastly, a work out plan of repayment is established with the homeowner

The lien is created

When a person wants to purchase a home, they may look to several different banks to what they can get for a loan. Each bank will require slightly different qualifications from the borrower. These qualifications will include, but not limited to, buyer pay history, credit score, length of employment, length of stay at current residence and much more.

Based on these qualifications the borrower may or may not be approved for a loan up to a certain amount and a specific interest rate. Once the loan is approved, the borrower will sign the agreement, legally binding them to paying the amount the bank loaned them backed by a mortgage on their residence. These loans normally last between 15 and 30 years depending on what the borrower chooses.

Again, the mortgage is the collateral tool used by banks. If the borrower would default on the note, the bank would take the home back as payment.

Most loans will include in the agreement specific items such as late payment charges and other typical penalties for non-payments and such.

Borrower Stops Paying, Lien No Longer Performs

Let's start with a real life example: Erik, a construction worker and a father of two, from Connecticut broke his leg on the job. He got laid off and can no longer make payments on his second mortgage, or so he thinks. His mother is helping him with the senior lien monthly payment on his home. Erik hasn't been paying for 3 years when our company purchased the junior lien. We asked him what happened, he told us his story.

We asked him what was happening now. He said he has started a small online, multilevel marketing, business and was finally making up to what he made while he was working in construction. We asked him what he planned to do with his second mortgage. He said nothing; he thought the bank wrote it off because he hasn't heard anything from the bank in almost three years. We told him that he was still delinquent and he owed us what he had agreed to pay on the original loan.

Borrowers like proof of who you say you are and the copies of the original paperwork. We will mail copies to each person we work with in the wake up package discussed in full detail in chapters to come.

This kind of example happens all the time. People get sick, they get hurt and move. Unexpected things can happen to anyone. This is why it is so important to ask them questions of what happened so you can step back and see a broader view of their situation. Keep in mind that we are in the business of working with second position junior liens, and usually the second is the first to be ignored.

Banks are usually willing to work with a person if they experience hardships; the key is to keep communication. Banks like when you can provide what happened in their situation. Banks may be able to slightly modify the loan.

Keep in mind; banks are in the business of loaning money, not reclaiming properties. It costs the bank money to reclaim properties such as taxes, foreclosure costs and other expenses. Usually banks would rather sell the loan at a discounted price than to reclaim a property.

The Lien is Sold

Have you heard of loss mitigation? We've had a glut of bad loans go through loss mitigation since the economic crisis of 2008. All these loans from the subprime mortgage lending went to these departments in big banks because the borrowers defaulted. This creates a massive opportunity for you and I. We get to buy these loans directly from the bank or buy them from the hedge funds who buy them from the bank.

If you choose to buy them directly from the bank, you must have deep pockets and serious connections with the heads there. Normally, I recommend buying them from hedge funds. You may have to pay a higher premium to the hedge funds, but you should still get a great deal on the note or pools you purchase.

A hedge fund a collective group of investors who pool their money together, lots of it, to purchase assets in bulk. Hedge funds sound big and scary, but when you really get to know them, there's nothing to be afraid of.

Like I said before, banks are in the business of lending money, so they do not want to keep non-performing assets on their books for long. They prefer to sell these assets,even at a loss, so they don't have to spend their resources on fore-closing on real estate.

Larger hedge funds usually come in and scoop them up for pennies on the dollar and resell them to us small inves-tors and keep the spread.

The lien is available for purchase to accredited investors and/or hedge funds

When hedge funds buy delinquent loans from the banks, they sell them either on a loan level basis or in pools. When you purchase a loan on a loan level basis, you are purchasing loans only one or two at a time. The hedge fund will send you a collateral file for each loan which includes the original note and mortgage, and the assignment and any other perti-nent information included with the loan.

Buying a pool is when you buy a collective sum of loans. Picture a large swimming pool that is filled with individual loans. If you bought a pool of loans, it would be like buy-ing the entire swimming pool filled with individual loans. These loans could be high or low in equity or somewhere in-between. Generally, you can get better deals when buy-ing in bulk/pools compared to buying loans on a one or two basis. Keep in mind that when purchasing pools, some of the loans could be really hard to work out, however, in most cases, you will have some nice high equity loans and make up what you paid for the pool from collecting the back pay-ments from the borrower in one loan.

When looking for hedge funds to purchase your notes from you will want to look for companies that have been in the business for a long time and have a great name for themselves.

We look to Partners for Payment Relief because we were mentored with them and have been with them for an extended period of time. They also warrant their notes saying they are what they are legit.

Hedge Fund Sells Lien to Individual Investor

Once hedge funds buy pools of loans from the big banks they will either split up the loans into small pools and sell them or they will keep the loans they want and sell the rest to small investors.

Hedge funds will mark the small loans up just a little to make selling them to us more profitable, but in most cases they will leave plenty of room for you and I to make money. Some of these hedge funds have business models to acquire these assets for a set price and then resell them quickly for a spread. They don't have the time to work out the loans. This is where the individual investor comes into place to work out the loan with the borrower and create a healthy passive income while helping them out.

You and I Buy These Notes

At this stage in the cycle, this is where you and I are most likely to buy the delinquent liens.

You have some options when you buy these notes. You get them performing, this means to work with the home-owner to get them to start paying back on the note. You can buy notes at a set price and sell them at a higher price to an-other investor, also called brokering notes. I am a buy and hold investor, it works better for taxes and I just like having checks coming in each and every month.

I've included what hedge fund I buy my notes from be-low. My brother, Mitch Hell, and I trained under Dave Van Horn of Partners for Payments Relief. These guys have been in the note business and have so lots of experience. I do rec-ommend their company for coaching and learning the basics of note investing. Note investing is really a learn by doing business.

Before you buy notes:

Before you buy any notes, I want you to raise $5000.00-10,000.00. I don't care how you raise this money. It can be your own or someone else's. You need to have some seed capital in this business. Let me break down what you need to raise the capital for. You will need to purchase a note. When you purchase the note, you will need to put the note into servicing which is like hiring a property manager to manage a rental property, which may range from $15- $40.00 per month. You may need to initiate your right to foreclose on the property which may range from $150.00 to much more depending on how far the foreclosure takes you.

As you can see, you will need some money when starting in this business. The last thing I want you do is dig into your savings, spend all you have to purchase a note and then have nothing left to further pursue the property if the payments are not made. We have seen that with some of our close friends, and it didn't end well for them. ***Wait until you have the money to begin investing and talk to a financial professional before starting!***

What's a good note and which ones do I buy?

This is the very first question I had when first starting in this industry. The answer is it depends on a couple things such as your risk tolerance, financial goals, and time.

I'll describe our ideal note and you can form your strategy from this.

I like notes that have a performing senior lien, and the equity spread between the fair market value and the senior lien.

Here's an example of a note with equity:

Fair market value of the property is $105,000

Senior Lien is $75,000

Junior Lien is $10,000

Equity between the fair market value and the senior lien is $25,000, that's a nice cushion should you have to foreclose on the property.

Having equity is the safety net for your loan because it protects your investment if the senior lien would foreclose on the property, you would get paid over and above what the senior lien was paid, in this case $25,000. Ideally, you want to purchase liens that have a fair amount of equity to protect your asset.

When the note has a performing senior lien, meaning that the borrower is still paying and is current on the lien above yours-1st position lien. More than likely the homeowner has emotional equity within the property and more than likely plans on staying in the home which means they will continue to pay the first or senior lien. When they continue to pay the senior lien, you have a better chance of getting them to start paying on the junior lien.

You can see all this information on the spreadsheet when you request it from the hedge fund. We get it on our email each month and purchase them on frequent basis.

NOTICE: Let me save you a ton of time and money with this valuable tip. Raise the money to buy good quality notes with the qualifications I just gave you. Never buy a loan without doing your research on it. You will see cheap notes usually under $2000.00, more than likely on these notes, the senior lien is delinquent. These can be very hard to work if you are just starting out.

When we first started, we bought an unsecured lien on a property in Pennsylvania. It was a mechanics lien in a divorce case. We didn't realize it was unsecured until about a week after we bought it. It was dirt cheap, only about $2800.00 with a payoff of about $15,000.00 due in 2021. The attorney representing the client says he's good for the money. Two years later, we sent the lien holder a letter requesting he only pay $5,000 to pay off his lien. We did this because we know the time value of money and didn't want to wait to see if he would pay since it was unsecure.

Point being in this story is to make sure that the liens you buy are secured by physical real estate so you are protected to the point of being able to take over the property if needed. By not having a secured loan, we can't necessarily do much if the guy doesn't pay. We can place a judgement against him, but it's more of a headache than anything. About seven months after sending out the letter, we received a check for $5,000. Thank goodness that deal worked out.

Moving On

When beginning in this business, although it is learn by doing, you want to purchase quality notes so you can get the cash flow ball going so you can reinvest those funds to buying more, eventually leading to financial freedom.

Matt's Preferred Hedge Funds

Partners for Payment Relief (PPR) http://pprnoteco.com

FCI Exchange http://fciexhange.com

Things to look for when buying Notes

Individual Notes vs Pools

When you first start in this business we recommend you start with buying one or two loans at a time. This is called *loan level* buying. You can focus on the notes that you have, develop creative strategies, and perfect your craft of working with homeowners. You can really choose the best loans with the highest equity.

On the other hand, pool buying is when a large or small amount of loans are bought at one time. Buying pools can be much more expensive and come with high, middle and low equity deal opportunities. You will have a very diverse portfolio when buying pools of loans.

In the majority of cases when you have the ability to purchase a pool of loans, some will be absolute junk, but, the other loans will pay off and cover the expenses of the junk loans and much more. You will need to focus on rehabilitating these loans to get them performing again. It will be worth your effort. Some of the high equity loans have massive payoffs. That's when you really have to celebrate once you structure pay outs with the borrower.

If you chose to be a pool buyer or a loan level buyer, make sure you research the loan of interest before you buy. If you are first starting, look for mid to high equity deals and make sure the senior lien is current. I suggest there be at least $10,000 – 40,000 in equity above the senior lien.

Here's some example deals with low to high equity.

Low Equity

Junior Lien Cost: $8900.00

Junior Lien Unpaid Principal Balance: $31,000.00

Fair Market Value of Property:$147,000

Senior Lien Amount:$135,000

Equity Above the Senior Lien: 12,000.00

Medium Equity

Junior Lien Cost: $5100.00

Junior Lien Unpaid Principal Balance: $75,000.00

Fair Market Value of Property:$128,000.00

Senior Lien Amount: $109,000.00

Equity Above the Senior Lien: $19,000.00

High Equity

Junior Lien Cost: $11,000.00

Junior Lien Unpaid Principal Balance:$38,000.00

Fair Market Value of Property:$215,000.00

Senior Lien Amount:$187,000.00

Equity Above the Senior Lien: $28,000.00

These loans may be in a higher price point, but are less risky and they provide the best chance for you to be successful on your first couple deals. Ideally you want to pick the loan that has the most equity to fit your investment needs.

Is the Senior Lien Current

Whenever you purchase notes on a loan level basis, you NEED to know if the senior lien is current or not. It will say on the spreadsheet if it is or not. Most spreadsheets will share if the senior lien is current, delinquent, in foreclosure or bankruptcy.

Senior Lien - Status	Senior Lien - Amount	Senior Lien - Reported	Senior Lien - Acc #	Senior Lien - Lender
Bankruptcy	$114,726	01-01-2015	200044612	BAYVIEWLSV
Bankruptcy	$1,460,000	11-01-2015	369131601	BSI MTG
Current	$406,896	03-01-2010	2000311385	SAXON MORT-GAGE SERVICE
Del 30	$122,500	02-01-2013	8655969336	OCWEN LOAN
Bankruptcy	$240,344	11-01-2012	1561024320574	CHASE MTG

Looking to see if the senior lien is current gives you a good clue to if the note is of quality or not. When the senior is current, the homeowners most likely has emotion equity in the property and more likely to work with you to pay off your second lien position.

Location

Keep in mind that if you need to foreclose on the property, you may own the property subject to the first position lien. What's *subject to the first* mean? Since the senior lien is still in a higher position than your lien you would have to pay them off first, usually at a very deep discount before you can claim the property.

Junior liens have very similar writing in them as the senior loan has. This means you can legally foreclose on the property if the homeowner does not pay you what they owe on the loan. You do not need the senior lien holder's permission to take back the property, however it is helpful to let them know what you are doing.

On a side note, keep tabs on the senior lien, meaning call them each month and to see if the homeowner is making payments on the loan. In our experience, on one of our notes, the senior lien was foreclosing and there wasn't a lot of equity in the deal and we nearly lost our investment because they were selling the house for what they owed the senior lien, leaving zero equity for us as the second position lien holder.

Look for loans on properties that are in good locations, meaning not by nuclear power plants or other weird places where most people wouldn't want to live.

You will be able to see the full address and county of where each of these notes are.

Long ago, our mentor Eddie Speed gave us some good advice. Here it is: "DO NOT BUY loans on single family homes near power plants, nuclear reactors or race tracks. If you wouldn't dip your kid in the water near it, don't buy it."

If you were to reclaim these properties, you will not be able to sell them. Keep that in mind when buying loans!

Price of the Note

I touched on this a little bit before, but I want you go have a better grasp on this concept. The price of the note really does closely represent the quality of the note. It's like a used car, if one is priced at $10,400.00 and the other $1,300.00, which one do you think had better reliability?

You can occasionally strike big on purchasing a relatively affordable note for under $5000.00 and reperform it, but its uncommon.

When looking at the price, you also want to consider the Fair Market Value (FMV), the Unpaid Principal Balance (UPB), Payment and Interest (PMT), and the Senior Lien. You want to know that you can recover what you paid for the note from the back payments and more.

Our *fast method* on researching what loans appeal to us:

Is the Senior Lien Current (Y or N)

Equity for the junior lien unpaid principal balance (UPB) = Fair Market Value (FMV) – Senior Lien

Examples:

Senior Lien is current

FMV: $210,000

Senior Lien: $175,000

Junior Lien (what you paid for the note) : $11,000

Equity for the Junior lien: $35,000

In this case, I would look into this loan because if the senior lien foreclosed on the homeowner, and sells the home, the senior lien would get paid in full and the junior lien would actually get paid in full and then some, so you can fully recoup your investment over and above of what the home is sold for.

In another example, I will show a lower equity spread deal

Senior lien is current

Fair Market Value: $492,000

Senior Lien: $453,000

Junior Lien: $36,000

Equity for the Junior lien: $4000

In this deal, with the senior lien being as high as it is and the fair market value a little bit above what this person owes, there's not much equity between them. If the senior lien was to foreclose on the home, you would get paid back what you paid for the loan but only to find that there is only a $4000 spread between them. Depending how how much the UPB is on the second position lien, I would stay away from this deal as there is little equity for you.

Moving on

If the equity of the junior lien is $5000- $10000.00 more than the amount we'd pay for the note, we'd look more into it.

When looking at equity on notes, notes will come in three buckets. The buckets are:

High Equity: These are the best notes. They will be a much higher price point for their quality, but you will have equity in the deal. Having lots of equity in the deal means if you were to foreclose on the property, you may be able to get the majority of the face value of you note.

Middle Equity: Middle equity notes are the most common. These notes will have some equity in them and be decently priced. When you first start in this business, these notes maybe in your price point. Usually if the senior lien is current, you have a much higher probability you can recover arrears and create a reasonable payment plan with the homeowner.

Low Equity: These loans are the bottom of the barrel loans. They are the cheapest and riskiest loans. Most likely the homeowner has buried themselves in a hole and you have to initiate foreclosure on the property immediately. Low equity loans are not necessarily bad loans to buy as we've had tremendous success with some of them.

When was the last payment on the note?

Most of the notes you purchase as a non performing junior lien will have the next payment backdated several years. I've seen them at the next payment due was seven years ago.

When the payments are way behind, and the senior lien is current, this may or may not affect if you can get the payments. This is when the emotional equity comes in. If the homeowners are in the home yet, they are more prone to working with you. If you were to purchase a cheap note and the senior lien is delinquent more than 120 days, you will have a hard time recovering those funds or working out the note.

What states to buy notes in?

First, you need to know each state's laws on foreclosure and bankruptcy. This information can be found in on the county website in which you are buying the note. Each state is different and you need to contact a real estate attorney practicing in that state for legal information.

Feel free to choose any state to buy notes in. We like to look to states that the real estate market is going up, so that if we had to take back a property we would have more built in equity for if that time comes. You can look on with a simple google search which markets are hot (home prices going up). I'm not opposed to buying in your own state if you are fortunate to. It gives you much more access to your property if you needed to connect with the homeowner or check out the property closer.

Personally I think the two worst states to buy notes in are New Jersey and New York. These states take FOREVER to foreclose on properties. My advice is to not purchase notes in these states.

Evaluate the borrower

Credit Score/Report: is this borrower generally responsible with their money? Look if the senior lien is current. Are they leasing or financing a vehicle. Have they been stable with a job? How much debt do they have, the more they have, the less they are able to pay you? Some hedge funds may let you see this information prior to buying the loan. All this is something you can look at to get a clearer picture of the borrower.

Does the borrower have a family or young kids? If so they may have more attachment to the property (emotional equity). Most families would rather work out a solution with you than be thrown out of their home of 15 years.

Investing in second position liens is more about working with the borrower than the property. You need to develop a trust with them and them in you. You want to be known as the investor who helps these people out and the one who can create a solution so they can stay in their home.

Purchasing the Loan

Here comes the scary part,but, once you feel comfortable with the note you are interested in, you've completed your due diligence, and are ready to buy, you will contact the hedge fund and purchase the note outright or place a bid with them. Most of these companies are very knowledgeable and will answer any questions you have. Try to build relationships with different hedge fund's asset managers so you can have the "in" with them.

Some companies will want you to bid and some you will be able to purchase outright. You will need to see what fits into your budget and strategy to decide what to purchase. Once your bid is accepted or you purchased your loan outright, you will receive a collateral file in the mail.

The collateral file will include the following documents:

Mortgage or Deed of Trust: The document draws out the conditions on what the money was loaned for. It will say where the property as collateral is located, that the property will be nicely maintained and insurance will be kept on it. This contract says if you don't pay, the lender has the ability to take back the property.

The Note: This document tells all the details of the financial terms including amount borrowed, when it's due and the payment each month. Always look for an original document with an authenticated signature. If you weren't provided with this, it will be recorded within the county it was taken from. Call the county courthouse and order a certified copy.

The Assignment: This is the document that transfers the right of ownership from the original lender to you. Make sure you record this immediately in the county where the note was purchased as it takes about 3 weeks for it to be recorded. There may be a nominal fee with this. Once recorded, you will look more credible with the homeowner about being the new owner of their loan.

The Accounting: The accounting comes from the previous servicer of the loan, all of which should be sent to the servicer that you chose to service your new loan. We recommend buying and servicing with www.fcitrust.com. The accounting will include the unpaid principal balance, payments and next due dates for the loan.

Tip when buying: When purchasing the loan, ask the hedge fund which company is insuring the property, you will want to add yourself as an additionally insured. If you are not on the policy, you may need to force place insurance on the home which can be expensive.

CHAPTER SIX

FINDING THE BORROWER

I hope you are getting a better grasp on what notes are, and how to purchase them. Now that you know this information it's time to take the next step.

Finding the borrower is critical to your success, and with success, is how you will get paid. Finding the borrower is like a game, you need to learn the game and exceed at it. Soon enough you will have the tools and steps to find them.

In most cases, because of the unique borrower's situation, they may be hiding from the world. In most of my experiences, the borrower keeps their curtains closed and don't associate with the outside world in fear that their home will be taken away. They dig a hole for themselves and don't let anyone in.

You are in this business to help people out and realize a profit for your services. Your goal is to find the borrower, listen to their story find create a workable solution for them to pay their debt back. The better you get at working with borrowers from finding them to creating solutions the more success you can achieve in this business.

When initially going after the borrower, we like to implement four key components. First, it's finding the borrower using several tactics. Second, we will uncover the homeowner's intent. Do they want to stay or move? Third, we will talk about a solution so it's a win win on both parties. Lastly, we will settle to an agreement to what they are going to do. We may structure a loan modification, or any other solution.

When trying to find the borrower we will send out a set of letters to their properties address. You will be able to find their property address on their credit report or the collateral file once you purchase the loan. Most of these letters were taught to us using Partner's for Payment Relief mentorship program. These letters work and that's why we are sharing some of this information with you.

#1 Letter: RESPA / Tila Letter

The first letter will be called a Real Estate Settlement Procedures Act (you can call this letter RESPA). Basically, it's a letter that says we will be servicing your new loan. It's communicating with the borrower what's happening to their loan and then they can stay in the loop. The hedge fund that sells you the loan will also be sending a RESPA letter out saying goodbye to the homeowner. You can search in your state website for a fillable form to send to your borrower. You will fill in the homeowners address, name and date it. Always make a copy for yourself, and send one to the ad-dress of the borrower.

#2 Letter: Homeowners Options Letter

The next letter we send will be a home owner's option letter. In this letter we tell of several options the borrower can choose from. These options will include a discounted payoff, a reinstatement program, sales assistance, and a cash for keys program. I will go over each of these for you now.

In the **discounted payoff**, just like it sounds, you as the investor will accept less than the face value of what is owed on the debt. Keep in mind you need to know what you paid for the loan and any profit you want built in. For example, if you had purchased a loan for $10,000.00 and the face value was $83,000.00. You would ask the borrower what can they pay you to satisfy the debt. You could settle for $50,000.00, cut them a deal saving them $33,000.00. And you would still make $40,000.00 on the deal. Negotiate something that will work out with the buyer. Always have all offers in writing with all parties signatures on them.

The **reinstatement program** will address the arrears that are owed on the note. Arrears are the back payments or missed payments on the loan. In most cases, purchases non performing notes will have some amount of arrears tied to them. These payments can be large or small, depends on when the borrower stopped paying on their loan. In any case, you can negotiate with them how much they will owe on the arrears. We like to talk with the borrower about the arrears and see if they can make any payments towards the arrears or even create a balloon payment at the end of the loan to address them.

Most cases will only provide you with collecting only a portion of the behind payments. You need to keep on the borrower to pay you the rest when they can or when you negotiate a predetermined timeframe with them. Always think, how this can be a fair deal for both parties involved.

The **sales assistance program** deals with the realization that the homeowner may need to sell their property. Their financial situation is over their head and their need to leave the property. This happens when the borrower lost their job and they are house poor. Being "house poor" means their mortgage payments are way too high than what they can handle. The best thing you can help this person with is helping them find a good realtor, moving company or anything they need help with. Your help will mean a tremendous amount with the homeowner.

Lastly, the **cash for keys** program is where homeowner hands you the keys and signs the home over to you for a small administrative fee. The fee helps them get back on their feet with moving and can range from $500.00 to $2500.00 depending on the value of the home. This money gives the person a fresh start and helps them to avoid a short sale or foreclosure on their record. You will want to contact a real estate attorney to complete this transaction of deeding their property to your name.

#3 Letter: No Response Letter

This letter is telling the borrower that you are still here to help them in their time of difficulty and are still obligated to pay their debt. You are reminding them that you own their loan and showing them what they owe. You will want to say in the letter to contact you in a friendly manner and work out a solution. You have to appear open and friendly, you don't want to appear like you are a stone cold bank.

#4 Letter: Billing Statement

You will be purchasing you loan through a servicing company that will manage all the accounting on the loan. They will provide you with statement of all the arrears and what the homeowner owes. You can send the person a billing statement of what they owe. This will be very official and most likely be the key to having the borrower contact you. They need to know you are official and have the power.

#5 Letter: No Contact Postcard

This is a postcard sent to the home saying that "We haven't heard from you, is everything ok?" It's a postcard so the person won't have to open official looking mail. The color of the postcard will be a neon color so it really "pops" and the person will definitely see it in the mail. Ultimately, you want the borrower to call you from the post card. Your call to action must be strong. In case you don't know what a call to action is, it's the message that says what you want the person to do. Call you!

Use these letters liberally because they have worked wonders for us several times. You need to be consistent when trying to contact the homeowner. Keep the pressure on them so they know you are serious about helping them. Once you scale up, and acquire more notes, you will want to automate letter sending to the homeowners. We use *Click2Mail.com* and let them send the letters. They have so many templates and pricing to meet your needs for this task.

Guerilla Marketing Tactics for Finding the Borrower

Private Investigator

Using a private investigator in the area you purchased your note may be a viable tactic for contacting the home-owner. Usually the investigator will have access to data services that can track where people are or have moved to based on their last known address. We use a web service for finding private investigators in any state. Go to www.pinow. com

Door Knocking Service

A door knock service is just like it sounds. It's a person who goes to the property where the note is attached to and will knock on the door to see if anyone is home. We use a company called Nationwide Management Services Inc. They usually charge around $300-$500.00 for their fee. If they don't reach anyone the first time they will go back to the property another day up to three times. You can google professional door knock service in your area or where you purchased your note.

Ordering Pizza

We had a borrower who was very, very hard to contact. Everything we did, he always avoided. We came up with, what if we have pizza delivered to his home. No one's go-ing to reject a college pizza dude coming to their home. We ordered from a local pizza chain restaurant from the com-fort of our own home in WI for a person in New Jersey. We ordered online so not a lot could be tracked back to whom ordered it. We know when the pizza was delivered as we got a notification over text that the pizza is at the doorstep of the home. Better yet it was confirmed that the person took the pizza as it was prepaid over the internet. We knew then that there was someone indeed living in the property. We send out a demand letter the very next day basically saying if you don't pay, you don't stay. We worked out a solution with him shortly after.

Reverse License Lookup

When I work with John Marsh, at Nationwide Management Services Inc., who conducts our door knock services, his agents take close up pictures of the owner's vehicle license plate. When I get a clear visual of the plate, I'll put that info into a service online that will look up the person's DMV records and in most cases you can collect their phone number. Try this method out and see how it works.

Delivering Flowers

We thought of this idea based on prior experience with relationships in our own lives. The best delivery services will make multiple attempts to bring the flowers to the designated person. If the person is not home, they services will try up to three times to try to make physical contact to deliver the flowers. All you have to do is search online for the best flower places in the area where the note was bought and tell the flower delivery service to call you when the flowers are accepted by the person living at the home. You will know then if there is a person living there.

Wake Up Package

The Wake Up Package is a strategy we learned from our mentor Gordon Moss. The package is designed to look official and get the home owners attention to contact you. The wake up package contains the following documents.

An introduction letter: This is a letter saying that we bought their loan and that they have a legal obligation to pay us and if they don't we have a legal ease to foreclose on their property if their end isn't fulfilled. The letter also tells them who we are as a company and how exactly to contact us regarding their loan. We like to include real testimonials from successful workouts with our previous borrowers for social credibility.

The promissory note (a copy of it): The homeowner will want to know you are who you say you are. Giving them a copy of their original note will give you that credibility. Usually you will have an assignment saying that you own the note. They need to see this as they may still think that they owe the original bank they took the loan out for. The copy of the note will have all the original terms and conditions spelled out.

Copy of the mortgage or the deed of trust: The mortgage or deed of trust is the collateral on the loan. The homeowner needs to know that the home is the collateral if they were to default on the loan, and you can take back the property if need be.

The demand letter: This is the letter, written by an attorney, saying "if you don't pay, you don't stay" in a nice way. The demand letter says what you want them to do. The letter will Formally request payment on your loan and how to contact you to go about it.

A video disk: The last item I like to include in the package before sending out is a video disk of me introducing myself, how I can help them, and how I have helped dozens of other homeowners. This video will set you apart from the bank and will give them a face of who owns their loan and aims to work out a solution with them. All you have to do is take a simple five minute video of yourself saying hello, and how you can help them and your plan to do it. Burn the video to a disk and save. Simple as that.

When sending the wake up package to the homeowner, you will send it either UPS or FEDEX or USPS signature confirmation. Sending the package with signature confirmation is the way you will know when the person receives the package and that they indeed received the package. You will want to hand write in big black permanent marker the person's address.

When you hand write the address and name, the chances of it being opened is much higher than using computer typed addresses. Let me ask you, would you not open a handwritten address package? Your curiosity would get to you and you would eventually open the box no matter who it's from. Same thing happens with the homeowner.

You've finally Contacted Them

Once you have contacted the borrower you will need to create a dialog with them and ask them three specific questions.

#1. What happened?

#2 What's happening now?

#3 What would you like to do?

These specific questions will give you and the homeowner an idea of where they are at and where they want to go. You can develop a solution based on the answers they give you. These questions will be explained in deeper detail later in this book.

You need to ask them if they want to stay or go. They need to make that decision. Help them understand what's best for them. Learn how to work out solutions with the borrower in the next chapter.

CHAPTER SEVEN

THE WORKOUT PROCESS

The workout process is where the magic happens in this business. In this stage of the game you are working out a solution with the homeowner.

Building Relationships with Borrowers

Participating in the note business is not all about the notes. Let me repeat this so you understand it, BEING IN THE NOTE BUSINESS IS NOT ALL ABOUT THE NOTES, IT'S ABOUT THE RELATIONSHIPS YOU BUILD. I need you to understand it. It will change your entire outlook on this business. You are going to be in the business of helping people create solutions to their problems. You are a problem solver, and if you're good, you are going to make lots of money doing it.

Whenever I obtain a new collateral file on a note purchased, I will immediately send the borrower a package that includes a copy of the original mortgage, deed of trust, and assignment of mortgage. Along with the paperwork, I'll send a personalized video on a disk for the person to pop into their DVD player called the wake up package I described earlier.

This video will have me talking and explaining who I am and how I intend to work out a solution with the borrower. I suggest you do the same. Make a video of yourself, explain who you are and be very sincere with it. Remember, you are developing a relationship with these people and you want to create trust through the video.

This video tactic works because the borrower is seeing who now owns their note and that they are willing to work with them.

Seeing the Big Picture

Before you can develop a solution for your borrower you need to get the big picture of where they have been, where they are at, and where they want to go.

You need to gather ALL the information including their story, their finances and all other aspects in their situation to formulate a solution to their dilemma. You're there to help them out of a financial situation and get them back on track to fulfilling their obligation to pay their lien.

For a successful workout for the borrower and yourself, you need to develop trust and rapport. The borrower needs to know that you care and they can trust you with helping with them in their period of hardship. Talk with them on a personal level. Remember, you can treat them differently, you are a problem solver.

As you are contacting your borrower of the note, you are going to ask them three questions. We ask these three questions to each buyer every time.

What happened?

This is where to get on the same page as your borrower. Ask probing questions like, what happened to get you in this situation. Did they get hurt or sick? Have they been through a divorce or job transfer or even laid off? You need all the details to create a mental picture of what happened with their finances and life. Your number one intention with working with them is to help them. You are trying to help them save your help and you are the one person who can solve this problem.

What's their current situation?

Learn what is happening at the present moment in the borrower's life. Again, asking questions is the best way to do this. Does the borrower want to stay in their current property or do they want to stay. Do they have a family and want to make their house a home. How can you help them with staying in their home?

What do they want to do now?

Ask the person if they want to stay or go. If they want to stay you need to give them options on how they can pay you. Everyone likes options; they feel they have choices when you offer them. Have an open mind when you offer options and consider all possibilities.

Being the owner of the note, you have limitless options on how to structure the payment plan. For example, you can make a balloon payment at the end of a specific time pay-ment to collect back payments or arrears if the person can't pay right away. You can bring the loan current by adding the back payments to the end of the loan payable later. You can really use your imagination at this. Consult a finance professional if you are newer to this industry before you present your plan to your borrower.

Putting it all on the Table

When you develop a trusting relationship with the homeowner, they will be more comfortable showing person documents such as personal accounts, statements and expenses. You will want to see all this to create a workable solution. Listed below are the documents you may want to see.

Income: You will want to sell all income sources from the homeowner. Check what they are receiving from a job, business, and any other investments. They shouldn't hide anything from you as you have the legal ability to reclaim their property if they don't pay you.

Expenses: We use a homeowner's financial sheet that helps us with listing all expenses the person may have. You can see this on the bonus file downloaded at MatthewHell. com/bookbonus Determining how much money is going out every month will give you a clear plan to what can be cut or reverted to paying you. Include everything such as bills, food, insurances and entertainment.

Financial statements: These statements will be from the person's bank accounts. Normally, every person will have a savings or checking with a local bank nowadays. If the homeowner has a spouse shares ownership on the property, you will want to see theirs too. Have the borrower print these out if they have online banking, or go to the bank to have them printed out.

Tax returns: Tax returns will give you an idea of how much they made from their jobs in previous years. Look for what they claimed for deductions to see if it looks legit.

All other debts: All other debts include credit cards, instalment loans, car loans, or any other liens against them or the property. If the person is in chapter 7 bankruptcy, and is successful at it, the unsecured liens will be stripped away. In case you're not familiar with secured and unsecured liens, secured is collateralized by something physical, unsecure is not. Keep in mind the more other debt that the borrower may have, the less they have to pay you. Try to work out a win win solution helping them pay off everything.

Credit reports: You should always receive a up to date credit report with the collateral file included when you purchase your loan. When looking at the credit report, it will list all debts and if they are delinquent or not. It will show all credit liens that are open or closed. The credit report will give you a wide view on the homeowner's credit situation.

Extra resources: Does the borrower have any extra income they didn't tell you about? Do they have a 401k or investments that they can draw from? Talk to them about family, can they borrower from any friends or members of their extended family? You need to think of out of the box sources of income. It will be to your benefit to help them with this.

Gathering all these resources will show you and the homeowner what they can or can't afford. The next step is to design a plan that fits into their budget.

Workout Action Plan Steps

Step One: Purchase the lien

This step is where you purchase your lien from a hedge fund.

Step Two: Finding and contacting the homeowner

As described in detail in chapter six, you have used the information provided to find and finally make contact with the borrower. At this time you have a dialog and are cultivating a trusting relationship with them.

Step Three: What's their circumstance?

You've asked if they want to stay or go. In this case, that would like to stay in the property. Using the documents described in this chapter, you've assessed their expenses and asked them what they can comfortably afford each month. You now know what they can afford for the arrears.

Step Four: The plan

Using the information provided by the borrower, you develop a repayment plan on the lien. Look closer at this real life workout deal:

1. $5200.00 payment for arrears to bring Jim's loan current.

2. Reduced interest rate from 7% to 4.5% for remaining term

3. Extended loan from 16 years to 25 years

4. Negotiated monthly payment is $425.00 for remaining term of the loan

Step Five:Share the plan with borrower

You will present this plan to the borrower for their review. If anything needs to be changed, go ahead and change it. Always have the borrower sign off on the changes. You have the ability as the lender to modify their lien for the benefit of you or them.

Step Six: Rewriting the loan modification

In this step, you will want to work with a real estate attorney to modify the loan; you're not necessarily rewriting it, you just modifying the terms slightly. Input all the information you discussed with the borrower. After all terms are agreed to, have everyone sign off on the terms.

Step Seven: Collect the arrears and monthly payments

Simply said in this step, you demand payment of all back payments. You should know how much they can pay from the financial information they shared with you. You may need to schedule payment of part of the arrears towards the end of the loan. The ball's in your court at this point.

As for the payments, you will share with the homeowner to pay your servicer, and then the servicer will forward the check to you each month.

Step Eight: Monitor the lien or sell the lien.

Your servicer of the lien will monitor the lien if it is current or not. They will let you know if the person is late on their payments.

At this point, you can enjoy your cash flow of the note. If you need more liquid funds to purchase another note, you may sell the note in the marketplace too. Selling a performing note will be much more lucrative than selling a non performing note.

These eight steps will be what you will do for most of your non performing loans. Some loans will be more difficult than others. You need to keep the pressure on the homeowner to pay you.

You have gathered all the necessary documents and know now that the homeowner wants to stay in their home. How are going to work with them?

Knowing you are not the institutional bank, you have many more options of thinking of creating options for workouts. The most common workout in our experience is payment plans. Usually we will negotiate how much they can pay towards arrears and then pay the rest via a payment plan until the loan is paid off sometime in the future.

When working with their finances, you don't want to make the payment to you outrageous, as the homeowner still needs money for other things. Paying too much on a mortgage is often called being house poor. Being house poor can be a nightmare in itself. Make sure the homeowner is comfortable paying you month after month at the same time.

Ask the borrower how much they can pay each month and if they can be consistent on it. Once you have agreed to an amount, get it in writing so you can keep them accountable. It's best to get everything in writing for legal ease.

Collecting the arrears

Arrears is the debt, or back payments on the loan that have not been paid yet. This debt builds up overtime and you are still allowed to collect it. This is you big money on junior liens.

These arrears will be shown in your accounting you receive from your servicer. If there are any late fees or other penalties, these will be part of the arrears too. Often, if the arrears are addressed promptly, this will be the first paycheck you receive. It will often cover what you paid for the note and maybe more.

Let me share an example with you. Say you purchase a small note for $6,000.00 and it hasn't been performing since 2009. Arrears and penalties on the loan accrued to $7200.00. You negotiate with the borrower to pay $6500.00 and agree to $148.00 per month until paid. With this likely example, you would have profited $1500.00 from arrears plus the $148.00 per month until the loan amortized. Because you now own the note, you have all the control to negotiate with the borrower,

In some cases, you will be able to attach the arrears to the end of the loan in the case of a balloon payment for a date in the future. Some borrowers will not be able to pay you a lump sum so quickly because of circumstances in their life. Ultimately, you are in control of how you want your money. Be creative with it.

Loan Payments

After you addressed the arrears with the homeowner, next is to see how much can they comfortably afford in monthly payments.

Using the documents to see their income, see what the person can afford each month. Keep in mind the borrower will need to eat and live yet, so be realistic with your numbers. I like to ask them "What's the most you can comfortably pay each month", and "Is that the best you can do?" Asking these questions will give you a ballpark idea of what they can do.

Extending their loan may be a creative idea. When you modify a loan to double its length, say from 15 years to 30 years, the payments will almost be cut in half. The interest rate may be more though. This may be the best chance for your borrower to pay you.

Doubling the time on the loan repayment will increase the amount of interest you receive and will help the borrower repay their loan. Again, it's a win win solution for both parties, what you always aim for.

CHAPTER EIGHT

DEALING WITH BANKRUPTCY

Bankruptcy has been a word commonly mentioned in our marketplace. It has become a negative or dirty word amongst newer investors. In this chapter, we will share how we as investors use bankruptcy to our advantage and how to stay on the right side of the law to avoid costly mistakes.

Case by case you will realize how to use the borrower's bankruptcy case to your advantage and how it can impact your results of success. As we've said before, this is a learn by doing business and the more deals you work, the better understanding you will gain of certain situations.

When we first began, like so many other new investors, we wear nervous purchasing loans that were in bankruptcy. We didn't know the difference between chapter 7 and chapter 13. By the way, these kinds of bankruptcies will be the most common you will experience in residential, single family notes.

Tell me more about Bankruptcy!

Mainstream media tells people that claiming bankruptcy on their debts will extinguish all they owe. People in these situations are usually at home with their head buried and the television is on. They hear an ad about bankruptcy and it ridding them of all their debt. This concept sounds appealing, who wouldn't want to run away from all their debt? Numerous people think they can get into mountains of debt and all it erased. And, this is simply not the case.

More than not, the majority of applicants applying for bankruptcy will not fully complete it due to misguided information and shady attorneys offering them a way out.

You will hear all kinds of stories from borrowers saying they may not owe you the money. They key is to educate the homeowner and bring them up to date to what they may not know. Let's make sure you know the difference straight away.

Two most common types of bankruptcy's

You will be dealing with Chapter 7 and 13 bankruptcies in this niche. If you venture out to commercial notes, seek legal advice to deal with that adventure.

An important point to mention is debt is either secured or unsecured. Secured debt is backed by real, tangible, collateral. You can actually touch the collateral. This debt includes notes backed by mortgages, vehicle notes, RV notes etc. Unsecured debt includes anything non physical such as credit card debt, medical bills. Unsecured debt is not tied to collateral.

Chapter 13

The most common bankruptcy you will be dealing with is chapter 13. As the individual goes through the bankruptcy, they will be appointed a trustee by the court. This trustee will help restructure the debt owed. This helps the applicant combine all the debt into one lump sum, and sometimes spreads it out for a longer amount of time so it's a lower payment.

When the personal files this type of bankruptcy successfully, they will be legally obligated to follow the plan for a certain amount of time. In our cases, the time is usually around 36 months, all the way up to 60 months.

Upon successful completion of this repayment plan, the borrower's debt may be reduced drastically or even removed all together.

The majority of people who file for this type of bankruptcy think their debt will go away, only to realize this is a repayment plan. They will get the help they need, and hopefully learn from their experience along the way.

Chapter 7

Chapter 7 bankruptcy is where the debt gets liquidated. All or most unsecured debt is wiped and like chapter 13, a court appointed trustee is assigned to them. The trustee is the resource to contact as they will be the ones paying the individual's creditors.

Why would one want to file chapter 7? They have no other choice. Circumstances in their life have led them up to this point, and at this time, they are giving up.

The person will be forced to sell basically all they have. This includes any and all assets, vacation homes, stocks and other investments. The trustee will be monitoring them highly that they are not hiding anything under their eyes.

Because chapter 7 erases unsecured debt you won't have to worry about your secured notes. The house holds the debt, and if the person wants to stay in the house, they have to pay the houses debt.

We use this line all the time with these clients. They think their mortgage is wiped, and they think their attorney told them it was. We ask them if they want to stay or go, then we say straight away if they want to stay, they need to pay the houses debt.

We like when our clients file chapter seven. Think about this, most if not all of their unsecured debt is erased. This includes credit card, medical debt etc. They cannot pay you more because they owe less to the other creditors. This benefits you to repay your note.

How can I monitor what's going on in the bankruptcy case?

We like to use Pacer.gov, stands for Public Access to Court Electronic Records. This is the source that you will use to find all you need to know about your client's case. You can login and join for free but viewing each page will cost you money. We recommend printing the pages you view since you are paying for them and file them away in each client's file.

You will be able to find out so much more than you already know about your client including incomes and other assets they may be hiding.

Keeping your distance

You want to keep your distance from calling and contacting the borrower when they are in bankruptcy. This is the time where they are working on repaying their debt that has accrued and getting their life back in order. If you need to reach out to the person for any reason, research which lawyer they are using and reach to them. They will provide you will the trustee appointed to the homeowner's case. Using Pacer.gov has really opened the door to monitor the cases online. It will save you time and energy by monitoring your bankruptcy loans monthly using the online database.

How does bankruptcy benefit you?

Like we stated earlier, when you start out in this business, bankrupt assets can be a little bit intimidating. Hopefully I can alleviate you of some of these fears in this section.

They start paying me

During a bankruptcy case, the defendant is assigned a trustee. The trustee is the person you contact if you have any questions about the individual's case. They are acting as the middleman.

The trustee will structure a payment plan with the homeowner in order to pay the lender back. The borrower may not want to pay you, but now they have no choice. The trustee will develop a court appointed repayment plan that the person must pay. If the borrower defaults, they get kicked out of bankruptcy and usually doesn't end will for them financially.

More Dough

Usually the payment is a little bit higher than their original loan payment when structured with the trustee opposed to what you may have collected if the person wasn't in bankruptcy.

You should always be available to work out a solution and try to help the borrower, but sometimes you need to make bigger actions. You may need to reduce the payment, set up balloon payment or restructure the loan altogether.

The trustee will be on the borrower to make their payments, so your life will be a little bit easier to focus on other notes.

The borrower's other debts have left the building

This applies to when the borrower successfully completes chapter 7 bankruptcy. Because Chapter 7 bankruptcy eliminates unsecured debt, they may have more to pay you off.

When the courts look at the borrower's debt, they will put them in two categories, secured and unsecured. Unsecured debt will be wiped away, but the secure debt will still be owed. I like to say to the borrower "if you want to say, you need to pay the houses debt." The houses debt doesn't get erased because it is secured, it's a physical asset.

When the borrower fails in bankruptcy

In most cases 80% or more of bankruptcy cases will fail. The borrower will not follow through with the plan from a variety of reasons.

They were offered help from the trustee, and yourself to create a reasonable plan to pay off their debts. It's not your fault they didn't follow through with their obligation, they made the choice not to.

When this happens you have the option of exercising your legal right to reclaim your asset. Foreclosure is the next viable option, which will be described in the next chapter in detail.

Taking the next step

Bankruptcy can be a valuable tool if used correctly. It can make your life easier and help the borrower repay their loans.

Utilize the trustee to the max to keep up on your assets. Don't be afraid to communicate to them about what's going on with their case and use Pacer.gov to keep track of the bankruptcy case.

Pay attention to the next chapter, foreclosure and the junior liens to see how you can use this tool to exercise your legal rights.

Hopefully this chapter helped you understand bankruptcy a bit better. If you still have questions, there are plenty of resources at your local library and real estate bankruptcy attorney's office.

CHAPTER NINE

FORECLOSURE AND THE JUNIOR LIEN

F oreclosure can be an exciting or scary topic to think about. In reality, if you need to use this tool, you are legally able to reclaim the property. However, it should always be your last resort.

The main objective to this business is to help these people stay in their homes and create a fair repayment schedule to you or your company.

There will be times you will have to exercise your legal right to reclaim your asset. I want to teach you how we've been successful at it. Here we go.

Case study

Keep in mind that all states are different, this case study is specific to New Jersey; be sure to check the state the note was purchased for full details on how their foreclosure proceedings go.

After repeated attempts to contact a homeowner in New Jersey and still no contact back,I knew I needed to begin foreclosure. I had tried all the tricks mentioned in previous chapters including the door knocking, pizza delivery, demand letter and such and still no response from him.

We had been going after him for about two months at the time and needed to turn up the heat so we could turn our money into a new note. Let me mention to you that we do not advise buying notes in New Jersey or New York! These states can take an upwards of two years to complete the process and are ridiculously expensive to do so. Avoid these states at all cost; I don't care if the notes are cheap or current on the first. Our mistake is your gain.

We had contacted a foreclosure attorney in New Jersey and told him we needed a demand letter sent to a specific property. He wanted us to send him copies of the collateral file such as the note mortgage, assignment and reinstatement letters etc. We emailed him the docs and he sent the demand letter and a copy to us the following Monday.

The attorney then started on the other steps on the process which included a title search, drafting the complaint, court filing and sheriff's service, judgment, writ of execution. All of this was going to be about $2000.00 at the time of this writing.

At this time we asked is there going to be any other costs for this foreclosure. The attorney mentioned we would also be responsible for any past due property taxes or municipal liens. So, as you can read, there were some hefty expenses with this note.

Thankfully, since we are not real estate attorneys, we let them to all the work and stood back while all the proceedings were happening. We were finally able to reclaim the property, subject to the first, about a year and a half later.

What! What's "Subject to" Mean?

Subject to is a word in this industry that means conditional or dependent on something else.

In this case study, there was a first position mortgage on the home, so once we reclaimed the property, we still needed to pay off the first lien. In this example, we contacted the lender for the first and negotiated a cash payout at a very deep discount. Usually if you offer cash, you can absorb an extreme discount.

Later we listed the home with a realtor in the area and told him that if he sold the home in 30 days he can keep twelve percent, sell it in 60 days keep eight percent, sell it in 90 days keep six percent. The realtor sold it in 30 days, and we were fully cashed out. The incentive of more money sure makes realtors dance and sell homes fast.

Using leverage in this industry is critical. Expand your social network nationwide, you never know when you will utilize some else's knowledge and connections. We have developed a spreadsheet of attorneys in each state that are preferred. Some were derived from our mentors at Partners for Payment relief. Be sure to keep this list updated as some attorneys move on to other practices or move to other states.

Why using foreclosure as a tool

The purpose of threatening foreclosure on a borrower is to try to get them to contact you and showing them the credibility that you have to exercise your legal right to recoup costs on your asset. You are essentially pushing the homeowner one last time to see if they will work with you.

The homeowner may be used to creditors mailing them direct mail, attempting to call and consistent threats of losing their home. What really happens is these are all attempts to have the borrower call them. The homeowner gets smart and if they aren't evicted after a year, most creditors lose credibly of working with the homeowner.

Before you foreclose on the home owner, you want to make sure you make all attempts to contact the homeowner. I like to send a letter from the Federal Trade Commission about the truths and options to avoid foreclosure. It helps to obtain a third party validation from a government website.

Listed are the things to do before foreclosing on the property

Recording the Assignment of Mortgage

Before sending a demand letter, your foreclosure attorney will need to know that the assignment of mortgage has been recorded in the county courthouse where the note is located. You should receive the assignment of mortgage when you receive your collateral file when you initially purchase the note.

Make sure to call the county recorder's office prior to sending out the letter and specifically ask them where to send it and how much the documents cost to record. In our experience, some recordings will be more expense and some cheaper. Make sure to find out the final numbers before sending the check for the documents to be recorded.

In some cases ,I acted too soon and sent a check to the recorder's office and didn't accost for postage to send the documents back. The county recorder sent the original paperwork and check back to correct the amount. This not only wasted about two weeks, but was double the postage to send it back on our end.

When you send the original paperwork, make sure to specify which assignment needs to be recorded first and second as some notes have been passed along though many investors. On a piece of paper, place your name and number so the recorder can call you if they have any questions. Lastly insert a self-addressed stamped envelope so it's easier and faster on their end to send back the paperwork to you.

Finding an attorney to send the demand letter

Attorneys will be state specific to where the home is located nationwide. Basically search the internet for attorney's in the state and research them. Call them to see what they specialize in. Make sure the attorney is indeed a real estate attorney and ask how many successful foreclosures they have participated in. Remember once you hire an attorney, they work for you. Make sure they are working hard for you.

The attorney will require specific paperwork for them to send the demand letter, most of which will have been included in your collateral file. Make sure you note is in servicing, as the attorney will need an up to date reinstatement letter for the homeowner. The reinstatement letter will spell out what the person needs to pay to bring the loan current again. Continue to follow up if the attorney needs any other information and paperwork.

Notice of sale is filed

Usually the attorney will take care of this, but you will always want to keep tabs on what they are doing. Open communication is a must and is critical to each property you have notes on.

The notice of sale is the intent to file a notice of selling the property within 90 days. In some cases lenders will sell the property for nearly what they paid for the property as foreclosing on a property is quite expensive. You will discover these costs when you initiate foreclosure on your own notes.

When filing the notice, you need to publish the notice in the local newspaper. Keep in mind you will need to publish the notice in the city the property is located. We've made the mistake of publishing a notice in another city, and had the hammer laid down on us.

The attorney will charge a fee for publishing the notice as will the space in the newspaper. Keep money reserves for these additional expenses handy, they may creep up on you eventually.

What's the notice going to say? The notice will simply say that the specific property is for sale. The ad will share the simple details of the property including that it's a foreclosure sale, and the place and time it will be sold at the auction.

The notice of sale step is most likely when you will have the borrower call you if you still haven't reached contact with them. Put yourself in their shoes for a second. You as the homeowner notice your home is listed in the paper for sale, in foreclosure! Your friends and family are probably calling you too saying what the heck is going on!

If you've had a diligent follow up letter campaign sent to the homeowner, they will most likely have your number and call you to see how they can stop the sale and how they can start repaying their loan to you.

The Property is Sold

This is the final step. The property goes to the foreclosure auction and is sold to the highest bidder. In normal circumstances, banks will become the highest bidder because they want to recoup some of their expenses they will lose in the process of foreclosing.

When the time comes to evict the homeowner, let the sheriff take care of all of that. There will be a lot of emotions in the situation especially if the whole family is involved and they have lived at the home for a long time.

You need to realize that you have given this homeowner all chances to work with you. You have sent the letters to show them you care, and want to work with them.

How long does foreclosure take?

Each state is a little different and you will realize this when you actually purchase notes nationwide. Like we mentioned before, we strongly encourage you to buy in states other than New York and New Jersey. These states drag the process out for about two years depending on what happens with the homeowner.

On the brighter side, if you do find a really good deal, and the senior lien is current, these states give you plenty of time to work out a solution with the borrower. One of our cases included a property in Paterson, NJ. The homeowner didn't contact us until the property was nearly sold at auction. Keep in mind that you can always stop the foreclosure until it is sold at the auction.

Common fears of our students

We've noticed many of our new students fear having to foreclose on the property. They fear all the paperwork and work associated with it. Many think they will have to go thru the whole foreclosure process.

You should know that in this business the chances of you having to sell the home on the courthouse steps is very slim. In most of our cases and countless experts can tell you that the homeowner will contact you ninety five percent of the time once they find out their home is going up for sale in the paper, especially if their senior lien is current.

We recommend using a credible real estate attorney in the city where the property is located in. Call the attorney so they know what you intend to do and keep good email records with them about the specific property.

Ask the attorney exactly what steps the state uses in fore-closure and the costs associated with them. You can then plan out your expenses for the note from the beginning of the legal action until it concludes.

Is the state Judicial or nonjudicial? Judicial is when the foreclosure goes through a court, and non-judicial is when it doesn't go through a court. Each can have their perks.

We can attest to quick closes in non-judicial states, but that doesn't give you much time to work out a solution with the homeowner.

Just to make this set in, in this business, you will nearly never have to complete the full foreclosure process on a bor-rower. Foreclosure is used as a tool, and sometimes may be your best and only option to have the homeowner contact you.

Working with the Senior Lien

The wording in the second position mortgage note is nearly identical when it comes to foreclosing on a property, but you need to understand that you will be "Subject to", the first position lien when you obtain the physical property. Like we mentioned before Subject to means that you need to payoff the first before you can own the property free and clear.

You will need to contact the bank or owner of the senior lien to cash them out or work out a reasonable offer to make payments to them. Essentially, you are switching roles from lender to the borrower when it comes to the senior lien.

You can find information on the senior lien usually on the credit report that will come with you loan file. They will have the number for the bank who hold the note. In most cases, you call the number in the automated phone line, enter in the borrower's social security number, and any other info and they will tell you the payment, loan balance and last payment made. This will give you an idea of what to offer to pay them off and how much you will owe them each month.

If you purchased the loan when the senior lien was current, you will want to call the lender each month and make sure the borrower is up to date on the payments. The owner of the senior lien does not have to tell you if they are foreclosing on the property.

Going further

Now that you have a better understanding on the foreclosure process you can move onto the next chapter about loan servicing. Loan servicing is to notes as property management is with physical properties. They are a third party who takes care of all the payments and accounting.

When you grow in this niche and your business expands, you may not be about to handle all the payment collections and accounting with each loan, so you will want to hire this out to experts to deal with these notes everyday.

CHAPTER TEN

LIEN SERVICING

W e've covered a lot so far in this book. Now, I want to teach you how to automate some of the work.

I will be covering loan servicing in this chapter and explain how it works and what company I have been working with. Most newbies do not understand the value of a loan servicer, but you will soon see the value in that a loan servicer has to offer.

When you buy a note and get it to re-perform, you will need to keep track of all the numbers and accounting. If you're like me, you will not want to do that because there's a lot of work and it's incredibly tedious.

Why work with a loan servicer?

When buying notes with most credible hedge funds, they will require you to purchase the note with a loan servicer. That way the hedge fund can transfer all accounting and booking with the loan.

When we buy our notes with Partners for Payment Relief, the loans will be bought with FCI Trust, a large loan servicer based in California. I recommend servicing the loan with FCI Trust because they have been in business for a long time and our mentors use them as well. They are very easy to work with too, and their fees are competitive in the market place.

Think of a loan servicing company as a property management company. Like in multi-family real estate, you need to maintain your properties; a loan servicer works the same way for a note.

A note servicer will become more valuable with the more notes you accumulate. They will keep track of all the records so if a borrower calls to ask about their amortization schedule, one can be produced at a moment's notice. The loan servicer will let the borrower know how much was paid on their loan, specific dates, accounting, and how much needs to be paid yet. You can request your 1098's from your servicer for your accounting prep work. When tax season comes around, accounting will be so much simpler for you too.

You can direct you borrower to call the loan servicer for any questions regarding the accounting on their loan. Make sure to let your borrower know the best number to contact them and refer to their loan number when they call.

Your loan servicer, you'll be the central hub of where you can monitor the status of all your loans. I like to call it the "back office", I can check when payments were made, if any are defaulted and print any type of receipt at my convenience. This comes in handy when you need to contact your servicing company about any particular borrower, you just have to call them and they can bring up their information for you.

Leveraging your time will be critical when you make it big. Time really is the most valuable asset in that you can't ever get it back. Thinking of how you can leverage your time will benefit you greatly. Focus on acquiring more notes, let the experts take care of everything else.

I have to notify you that the loan servicer will not be the one working out a payment plan with the borrower. This is your job, this is a very high touch business, and you will be the one to do this. Don't rely on the servicer to do your dirty work.

A few servicing companies may help you with collections for a very high fee. You need to watch out for how they do this because most will automatically foreclose right away before learning the borrower's situation.

When a servicer automatically forecloses, quality relationships don't develop and it's not a win win situation. So all in all, I don't recommend you consider services like these.

Self-Servicing Notes with Note Smith

You may not have a lot of notes or feel you can handle servicing loans yourself. Note Smith loan servicing software can help you do the servicing yourself. As of this writing in 2016, the Individual package for the starter investor is around $299.00 plus fifteen dollars shipping and handling. You can purchase the software at NoteSmith.com

Note Smith will provide you with the software to keep track of each loan. You will track when payments were made, the current loan balance and much more. It was created by a note investor to keep track of his own loans. Check http://www.notesmith.com/ out for more information.

Whether you choose to use a servicer or self-service your notes, keep in mind your time is very valuable and should be taken seriously. Never settle for the first servicer you find, use one you trust and feel comfortable with.

If you're looking for ways to grow your wealth and profits tax free and under the protection of a Roth IRA, keep reading. The next chapter will share how you will benefit from using IRA's to grow your retirement nest egg.

CHAPTER ELEVEN

SELF-DIRECTED IRA NON PERFORMING NOTES INVESTING

Congratulations for getting this far in this book. I am proud that you have kept reading and now know how working with borrowers can build you a fortune. Now is the time to start thinking far into your future and look at ways to keep the money you've made. I will be sharing how I started generating money with notes with a Self-Directed Roth IRA.

Before we begin talking about the IRA, let's talk about taxes. As will most any investment, you will be taxed unless it is in an non taxable account. Let's say right now, you have 10 notes that you have begun to re-perform and you are currently collecting $450.00 per month, per note.

Number's Recap

10 Re-performing notes

$450.00 Average payment per note to you

$450.00 x 10 = $4500.00 per month

$4500.00 x 12 = $54000.00 per year

Having a Gross income of $54,000.00 may put you into a higher tax bracket, but what if you have larger goals and want to invest more and raise your income? You can buy more notes by reinvesting a portion of your income.

I want you to think about your future and future taxes. You must think, the more you make the more you must pay to Uncle Sam. If you want to avoid taxes keep reading.

Traditional IRA

While the majority of people know and use a traditional IRA, this IRA may not present benefits for the real estate investor. Basically, the traditional IRA won't be as effective of the other IRA I will mention next.

Typically with a basic IRA, all you have to do is put the allotted amount of money each year into the account and save for the future. Our tax code allows for taxes to be taken out when you withdraw the money at age 59 ½. Usually the investing work is left to the IRA custodian and/or manager, which sometimes may not be in your best interest.

Although I do recommend anyone to have an IRA, specifically for investing in notes, this type is not your best option. Keep reading to learn about the self directed IRA.

Self Directed Roth IRA

Let us talk about how to continue building empire tax free. At this point you may have bought your first note, if not that's ok too. Look about ten or so notes into the future and say you have them performing, what may you want to do with the future notes you buy? As long as you have all your living expenses covered, I would suggest buying them with your IRA.

What is a Roth IRA? A Roth IRA is an individual retirement account and I believe it is the best way to save for retirement buy buying investments in it.

As my Equity Trust Company IRA Custodian would say *"A self-directed IRA puts you in the driver's seat of your financial future, giving you the freedom and control to invest in assets you know and understand best. The power of a self-directed IRA comes from the almost endless investment options. You are not limited to just stocks, bonds and mutual funds – you can invest in real estate, promissory notes, tax liens, private businesses, precious metals, etc. Plus you reap the asset protection and all of the tax advantages that come with government-sponsored retirement plans."*

The money in the Roth is taxed before it goes into the account at the current tax rate, this way, when you take it out at 59 ½, you will have paid your taxes and won't have to worry about them. You won't have to worry about being in a higher tax bracket and will end up with a larger retirement fund when it's that time to retire.

Listen up! The profits made by your Roth IRA's investments will not be taxed and will be under the umbrella of protection that the IRA offers. Can you imagine how many deals you can do when you know you will not be taxed? You can even flip deals in the short term and avoid the short term tax gains!

So, Matthew, When should I start a Self-Directed Roth IRA?

Have you ever heard the saying, "When's the best time to plant a tree?" Twenty years ago right? When's the next best time? Today!!

I recommend start planning retirement as soon as possible. Think for a moment, do you really think there will be enough money to support the millennials with social security. I like to say, most people will be in social insecurity when they retire, if they ever will.

Normally when happens is the average note investor will purchase a few notes starting off, sort of like what we did. Two will work out, pay you profit, and the other one may be a little harder to re perform. With the profits you will want to buy more notes to play the game again. Sooner than later you will reach your income potential and move up in tax brackets.

Just think, the sooner you open a self-directed Roth IRA account, the sooner you will begin to build your empire. I started my Roth IRA at age twenty three, placed about $5500.00 in it and began to purchase small notes. All the profits kept building and now have over six figures and counting for retirement. At this rate there will be seven figures in my forties.

Just know, it is entirely your choice to use which ever IRA you feel comfortable with. Consider the benefits of each with a specialized representative at a qualified custodian before you're finally choose which IRA you want.

You may have just fallen off your chair buy what I just said. I can understand that, as I was the same way when first learning this information. Thankfully I had Equity Trust Company to answer my questions. I have built a solid relationship with this IRA Custodian for numerous years.

You can find them here: https://www.trustetc.com/ or call 1-888-ETC-IRAS (382-4727)

Practical Example

A number of years ago, I was able to cover most of my living expenses with notes, including cell phone, mortgage, groceries, etc. I had reinvested a portion from each note to purchase new ones and was very satisfied with where I was financially in my life.

I still wanted to have plenty of money for my retirement but didn't want to pay Uncle Sam my hard earned money. So I started purchasing notes within the Self Directed Roth IRA. All you have to do with this is once you open an account with an IRA Custodian; you would fill out a self-directed investment form to buy the investment. Nice thing about Equity Trust Company is I make them to everything for me so I can focus on making more money.

Consult a financial accountant for complete details and advice before investing notes in a retirement account.

CHAPTER TWELVE

INVESTING IN PERFORMING NOTES

I purposefully left sharing with you how to invest in performing notes until the end of the book because i wanted you to learn the fundamentals of working with non performing notes before we got into the easier stuff.

Working with performing notes has been very rewarding for me especially after my mentors taught me how to work the harder notes. The advantage with performing notes is that the homeowner is already paying on the loan. All you have to do is purchase the loan you see fit, place the note in servicing, and cash the checks as they come to your mailbox each month.

Higher cost of entry

Typically investing in performing notes can mean a higher cost of entry when entering the note space. The notes we generally purchase that are already performing cost between $20,000.00 and $30,000.00. That can be a bit spendy for most newbies.

We started of in the non performing note space to acquire capital to buy more of these larger performing notes. I'd recommend if you want to make note investing into a full time career, invest all your payments and payoffs your receive from the notes for the first couple years at least. Remember, you are trying to create more freedom in your life. Reinvesting your profits will allow you to buy more notes and receive more income.

Where can I buy Performing Notes?

You can generally purchase performing notes from the same hedge funds you are already buying your non performing notes from. We continue to buy ours from Partners for Payment Relief. They warrant every note and we've build a strong relationship with Dave Vanhorn within the last several years.

Some hedge funds will sell these notes on a bidding basis, kind of like the non performing notes. Before bidding you must do your due diligence just like would when purchasing a non performing notes. I've come into some cases where it was a really good deal, the numbers were on, however the property was in a bad location. If that note were to ever default, and worst case scenario, i had to foreclose, that property must be able to resell at a profit.

Note Servicing

In most cases, servicing performing notes will be considerably less expensive than non performing. This in turn, gives you a much more generous profit at the end of the day. As of this writing, we pay FCI Trust $15.00 per month per note. That's not a bad number considering they take all the calls and accounting for each note. That's less headaches for us and more time acquiring more profit generators.

The nuts and bolts on how to make money, quick money from performing notes

I didn't start with performing notes, but had an idea one day about how to work them. Remember when I mentioned in the beginning of this book that this was a high touch business? Meaning you need to be nice and different than banks when working with home owners. Its the same way when working with these notes.

One morning, after continually trying to contact a specific homeowner in Florida, a thought came to me. What if I could use some of the capital I've raised from previous note payoffs and purchase a performing note and workout an early payoff with the homeowner?

I was thinking about this for about a week, trying to figure everything out before I approached Mitch, my brother, to tell him about the idea. He asked how much of a discount would you give? I said, we could set the rules because we own the note. I just make a rule to include a minimum margin of $10,000.00 per note regardless of the price.

I'll give you an example. Let's say there is a performing note, second position, in Tucson AZ bidding for $38,000.00. It still has 176 payments of $460.52

Tucson, AZ

Fair Market Value: $190,398

Senior Lien: $225,665

Senior Lien: Current

12 Month Internal Rate of Return (IRR): 13.52%

Monthly Payment: $460.52

Payments Remaining: 176

Amortization Payoff: $81,051.52

In this potential deal, there is equity above the senior lien, so if we had to foreclose, we could recoup some of our money. We would purchase this loan, send a series of letters to the homeowner, and convince them that paying the lien off early at a discounted price would be best for them. We could receive a payoff of $50,000 and save the homeowner just over $31,000 and will profit $12,000.

Moving on, I wanted to make working on these notes easy, easier than the nonperforming notes. Remember this business is about creating freedom, so operations must be optimized to be efficient as possible.

I wrote a series of five payoff letters that are sent to the homeowner after the transfer of ownership has been completed and servicing is in place. These letters are provided to give the homeowner a push to payoff the loan with a predetermined discount that we come up with. I want to *move* my money and turn it so it keeps making me money so time is of essence in this business. These letters for performing notes can me found on the book bonus section of Matthewhell.com/bookbonus

Giving a discount to the homeowner is a win win situation. Maybe you are already in a similar situation where you have taken a loan from a bank for a home. The bank gives you a discount on the payoff because they need more money to make more loans. See how this works, and homeowners are loving what we have to offer!

If they don't want to pay off their amount, we will continue to accept monthly payments at the normal interest amount until the loan amortized. Both are profitable scenarios, we just like the early payoffs more.

What happens if the payer defaults on the loan? Well, thank goodness you learned in the first part of the book how to rework with homeowners to get them paying on a non performing note. You may also choose to foreclose on the homeowner if they don't want to work with you.

In summary, there is opportunity in both non performing and performing notes. Mitch and I have worked both and like to work performing notes more because they offer less hassle and it works best for us as a lifestyle business. I value spending time with my family, girlfriend, traveling, and this business is perfect for our situation.

Final Words

You have made progress throughout this book. You have learned what notes are, how to buy them and work with a borrower. Now is the time you need to take action.

I cannot do this for you; you must take the first step. You must gain the confidence to do this. This is a learn by doing business. It is not easy; you will have hurdles to overcome. I can say that it will be every bit worth it in how you help these borrowers out. Remember, you are their last stand between them and losing their home. You have the ability to help them regain footing on their payments and have them stay where they are at.

Make it happen my friends!

"Take Massive Action, Get Massive Results"

–Matthew Hell

For Questions and Guidance please visit www.MatthewHell.com/bookbonus

ABOUT THE AUTHOR

Matthew Hell began his real estate career in 2010 as a wholesaler in Minneapolis/St. Paul, MN.

He has studied under the masters of real estate that include, but not limited to, Ron Legrand, Eddie Speed, Gordon Moss, Dave Vanhorn, Kent Clothier, and Robyn Thompson for over six years.

Matthew primary focuses on his portfolio of real estate notes and properties and enjoys helping people through hardships and creating a bright future for all parties involved. He believes this is the best time to be in real estate because of the surge of delinquent, second position, liens that defaulted from the 2008 housing bubble crash.

He has shared the stage with his brother, Mitch, speaking on many topics of real estate investing, personal finance, and has co -written several publications on the lucrative business of real estate investing.

In his free time, Matthew, enjoys traveling, mentoring aspiring real estate entrepreneurs, spending quality fun time with his family, beautiful girlfriend, and friends. As a way of giving to the community, he will frequently teach free real estate seminars as he appreciates how much his mentors taught him.

Visit MatthewHell.com/bookbonus to receive FREE Resources to start investing in Notes

www.ingramcontent.com/pod-product-compliance
Lightning Source LLC
Chambersburg PA
CBHW021433170526
45164CB00001B/217